Also by Tony R. Lindsay
from Indigo Sea Press

Lucas Lee, His Forebears and Descendants

Indigoseapress.com

Tattletale Roadhouse

and Social Club

By

Tony R. Lindsay

Gathered Thoughts Books
Published by Indigo Sea Press
Winston-Salem

Gathered Thoughts Books
Indigo Sea Press
302 Ricks Drive
Winston-Salem, NC 27103

First Gathered Thoughts Books edition published
February, 2016
Gathered Thoughts Books, Moon Sailor and all production design are trademarks of Indigo Sea Press, used under license.

For information regarding bulk purchases of this book, digital purchase and special discounts, please contact the publisher at
indigoseapress.com

Cover design by Tracy Beltran

Manufactured in the United States of America
ISBN 978-1-63066-187-8

I wish to acknowledge the contributions to this book of Tom Seaman and Carol Roan. Tom has been my advisor from the moment I mentioned the idea of writing a book. Carol has been invaluable to me with her critiques and recommendations.

Table of Contents

The Angel Of Ludowici	1
Wampus Cat Queen	7
Wilson's Dream	15
That Dog Will Bite You	19
Like You Never Heard	21
The Tattletale Roadhouse & Social Club	25
Forget My Soul	29
Mud Duck And Nimrod	33
Hawkshaw Hawks And Hog Albright	37
Melanie Burber's Christmas Letter	41
Wilma	45
Clyde	49
No More About Junior	53
Oddwater	59
No Talk	61
December Days	65
Back To Budapest	69
Ivory Blue	71
Never Gonna Make It	75
Kitty Green	79
Orchestra Music	83
Viagra For The Soul	85
Full Circle	89
Gone But Not Forgotten	91
Ol' Possible	93
Pretty Darn Clever	95
God Bless Miss Finch	99
Attitude	101
Nobody Ever Tells Me Anything	103
Where To Look	105

Table of Contents Cont.

Grandma, Speak To Me	109
Sweet Reason	113
The Noble Snake	115
Chinese Math	117
No Derby For Me	119
Sleeping With A Lightning Bug	123
Slowly-And In Ones Please	127
We Owe It All To Ugg	129
Getting Older	133
Carlos And Red	135
Ol' Dave	137
Wondering	141

THE ANGEL OF LUDOWICI

Twelve-year-old country boys, Homer Guthry and Elwood Hatmaker, had more in common than tattered clothing and enjoying the adventures of growing up in southern Georgia. They had a devoted interest in girls, especially for a statuesque brunette with stunning blue eyes—the lovely Veronica Hightower. Two years older than Elwood and Homer, Veronica was mature in mind and body. She wore expensive clothes and took private piano and voice lessons.

The Hightowers were prominent members of the First Presbyterian Church of Ludowici, a town of 1440 souls located along the west bank of the Altamaha River. Elwood and Homer arranged to be in town at noon on a Sunday when the congregation filed out of church. The boys observed the procession from a low stone wall. Elwood kept an eye peeled for Veronica as he whittled a birch block into the shape of a raccoon.

Most of the crowd had drifted to their cars when Veronica finally appeared. The boys scrutinized Veronica's every move from the church door until she was sequestered in the family's large, black sedan. Elwood and Homer giggled and elbowed each other.

"She's damn beautiful," sighed Homer.

"Hell, she's better than that. She's whatever is better than beautiful. Did you see her smile at that stupid preacher? Do you think he knows she's so pretty?"

"Naw, I don't think so. Preachers ain't like that. They just think about the Bible and doin' a bunch of good stuff."

"I ain't so sure. He'd have to be deader than roadkill not to see that she's the prettiest girl in Ludowici, maybe the prettiest girl in the world."

Elwood tugged his suspenders. "I wish we could see more of her. You know what I mean, see her more often than just a few minutes on Sunday."

"Yeah, I hear ya."

Elwood moaned. "Even her name is beauteous. It makes me weak. Do you reckon there's ever been an ugly girl named Veronica? Her mom and dad must have known with the first glance at their baby daughter that she was gonna be special, and they said, 'Let's

1

Tony R. Lindsay

name her Veronica.'"

The following Tuesday, Homer received the best news of his life from no less an unimpeachable source than Lefty Goins, proprietor of the Tattletale Roadhouse & Social Club and the local purveyor of strong drink. "Hey, kid, I hear you and Elwood are in love with that Hightower girl." Lefty threw back his head and made a howl like a wolf. "You fellers might as well wish for the moon. I guess you know that she's gonna be a special guest at Mount Harmony on the third Sunday in September. She's gonna sing and play a damn piano. Give them Baptist bastards a touch of class."

"Yeah, no shit."

Homer rushed to give his friend the lowdown.

"That's damn good, Homer. We can see her when she goes into Mount Harmony and see her again when she comes out."

Homer's eyes squinted and his lips slanted into a wicked grin. "I'm thinkin' way better than that."

"Whadda mean?"

"I figure we can go to church just like regular folks and watch her play and listen to her sing."

Elwood rubbed his hands together and bounced around like a puppy. "Hell, I'd be happy to watch her breathe. But we don't go to that dumb church. We don't go to any friggin' church. They wouldn't let us in the place and, even if they did, they'd know we was there just to see Veronica."

"I've thought about that."

"You have?"

"Elwood, you know I'm smarter than you, right?"

"Yeah."

"Well, here's what we're gonna do. First of all, they got to let us in when we show up at the door. Momma said it's a church rule. We'll go to Mount Harmony beginning the first Sunday in September. After a couple of weeks, nobody will notice when we're there the third Sunday to hear Veronica sing. Won't that be funner'n hell?"

"Homer Guthry, you're damn smart. Sharp as a rat turd, that's what you are. Let's do it!"

"Now listen, Elwood, let me do the talkin'. Remember, them are nice people. Them folks ain't like you and me. They call each other Sister and Brother even though they ain't no kin at all."

2

"Dumbest thing I ever heard."

"That's why you got to let me do the talkin'. I know more about sayin' stuff like Praise the Lord. Momma said they say that a lot. But I ain't gonna wave my arms and shout and carry on."

"Homer, you're sharp as a reindeer's peter."

"Yeah, damn right."

Homer and Elwood, dressed in their best bib overalls, shirts buttoned up to their necks, clean boots, and hair slicked down with axle grease, appeared at Mount Harmony on the first Sunday of September. Two sturdy men and a prim lady met them at the door and looked the boys up and down. Then they broke into wide smiles and extended friendly handshakes.

Homer responded to the hearty greeting by replying, "Yeah, and a good mornin' to y'all."

Elwood got a warm welcome to which he offered a tentative, "Praise the Lord." He received another greeting and responded louder, "Praise the Lord."

Homer gave Elwood a disapproving glance. The boys sauntered about halfway down the aisle, and settled onto a pew.

The sermon included several references to the gathering of sheep. Elwood whispered to Homer about the meaning of almost everything, especially the part about sheep. "What you reckon he's gonna do with all them sheep?"

"Dunno, but he's mighty keen on getting his hands on some sheep, and he don't care who knows it. And them church ladies smilin' and noddin' like they knowed it all along."

Elwood shook his head. "The man's got no shame, I can tell you that."

The lengthy service wound down and the boys made their way out of church. Several persons thanked them for joining the group in worship.

A hefty lady in a polka-dot dress beamed at Elwood. "Young man, we're so glad you are here in God's house today. I bet you have a sweet family."

"Oh, hell, yeah, you can book it. Momma's as good as they is anywhere. But Daddy's crazy about sin and the Widow Murphy."

"Ouch! Homer, that hurt."

Homer smiled up at the polka-dot lady as she clasped a hand over her open mouth.

Tony R. Lindsay

The second Sunday in September found the boys again at Mount Harmony. The preacher announced that the topic of the sermon would be "Lot's Wife." He related the Biblical account of Lot leaving the wicked city of Sodom, along with his wife, on the day the city was destroyed. Against God's command, Lot's wife looked back on the city and the pleasures she was leaving behind. Zap! She was struck dead and changed into a pillar of salt. Elwood licked his dry lips.

After the service, Elwood had several questions for his friend. "Did Lot have another name? Did Lot's wife have a name of her own? What in hell was goin' on in that place that was so bad?"

"Elwood, I ain't sure what they was doin', but whatever it was, it must have been awful damn good to be so bad. The point is, God'll strike anybody dead if they don't follow a straight-out command."

Another week passed as the hills and lanes of Long County were transformed into a canopy of reds, yellows, golds and greens. Maple trees seemed to shout, "Hey, look at me."

At last, it was the third Sunday in September. Homer and Elwood arrived early at Mount Harmony. They wanted to get a seat as close to the pulpit as possible.

Musical equipment in the country church consisted of an ancient pipe organ. But that Sunday an elegant grand piano had been positioned on a three-foot high platform especially constructed for the occasion.

With a groan, Elwood eyed the piano bench where the scrumptious Veronica would sit. "Lucky bench."

"Hush up, Elwood. Damn your ass, anyway."

The boys turned around to see the object of their devotion as she pranced along in high heels and took a seat two rows behind them. Veronica was even prettier up close. Her dark hair cascaded over her shoulders and onto a white dress with a lacy collar. Her bodice provided a hint of her high, youthful bosom; almost more than poor Elwood could stand.

The pastor announced that the day would be special for the good people of Mount Harmony. Miss Veronica Hightower would worship with them by playing her very own piano and singing a medley of her favorite hymns.

Veronica sashayed down the aisle and lightly ascended six steps up onto the platform. Her knee-length dress swung rhythmically left

4

and right, left and right, left and right.

Veronica smoothed her dress down the back of her legs and sat down on the bench as if she were about to sit on an egg.

Homer swallowed hard.

Elwood used the back of his hand to wipe drool from the corners of his mouth. "Oh Lord, she's gotta have a light in her head behind them blue eyes. Homer, you know I ain't never been outside Long County, but you can trust me on this—girls don't get no better nowhere in the world."

"Damn straight. Think about it. Millions and scads of women and none of 'em any better than the Angel of Ludowici."

Veronica began with "Peace in the Valley." She wowed the congregation for two minutes before the church was rocked by the sound of timbers splitting. The forward edge of the platform gave way, dividing the stage into two sections. The heavy piano slid toward the rear, spilling Veronica off her bench and onto her head between the two halves of the collapsed platform. Wedged into the crevice, she began to yell and struggle. Her feet flailed straight up in the air, but the more she maneuvered, the deeper her torso sank between the planks. The hem of her dress fell to her waist, exposing long shapely legs and gleaming white panties stretched over two perfect globes. Homer and Elwood's eyeballs stood on stems.

One woman and a score of men rushed to assist Veronica. The preacher bounded onto the pulpit and commanded everyone to look away from Veronica. When his instruction had little effect on the audience, and zero effect with Homer and Elwood, the preacher exclaimed, "Look away this instant, or God will strike you blind!"

Recalling with horror what had happened to Lot's wife, Elwood and Homer clasped both hands over their faces and lowered their heads. They could see nothing.

Elwood nudged his friend. "Homer, I'm gonna risk one eye."

WAMPUS CAT QUEEN

"Homer, ain't you scared 'bout what we're gonna be doin' when the sun goes down?"

"Naw, it takes a lot to scare me."

Homer had permission to spend the night at Elwood's house. Elwood's mother believed he would be sleeping at Homer's place.

Clouds played peek-a-boo with the sun on a breezy spring day in the foothills around Ludowici. Rhododendron blooms of white, pink and brilliant red spilled over the rocky outcrops and cascaded down the slopes.

Homer and Elwood had spent the day at a bottomless swimming hole known as Blue Deep. They'd chunked rocks at squirrels, and birds, and creatures that appeared and disappeared in the imaginations of twelve-year-old country boys. Joy gave way to apprehension as the sun sank behind dark purple mountains.

"Tell you what, Elwood. There ain't another two boys in this here county with the courage to do what we're gonna do."

"No crap, paleface. There ain't another two boys in the world stupid enough to walk the Cove Road at night."

The Cove Road was a centuries-old wagon trail with two deep ruts. The route forded ankle-deep streams, wound over low hills and bent around tight curves in a sixteen-mile loop surrounding a valley of lush farmland dotted with log houses and barns.

The boys were not inclined to think about how their bucolic glen was formed in the midst of rolling hills, but one explanation for the cove was that God pressed an enormous thumb down on the peaks and left a print of gigantic proportions. Each little ridge running through the pastures and fields was a line in a divine thumbprint. A less satisfying notion was that the almost flat cove with towering summits on all sides was created during the last Ice Age.

The idea for walking the spooky Cove Road at night was another of Homer's brain-lapses. But this one terrified Elwood because of the creature known to roam the cove—the dreaded Wampus Cat Queen.

Legend had it that the critter was a human-sized cat that walked upright and had the hands and feet of a woman. She had one horrible, yellow eye. And one sagging breast in the middle of her chest.

Tony R. Lindsay

Dagger-like teeth dripped saliva on her single, blood-stained bosom. The Queen had stringy, matted hair and warts and cankers everywhere. All this ugly had the slinky walk of a woman in heels.

Some folks said the Queen had mating on her mind. Woe, shudder and dread to the man who disappointed her. Paley Wilcox said, "It'll take a better man than me to hump that she-devil. The bastard would have to be blind, and hornier than a two-petered billy goat."

Usually content with a diet of deer and bear cubs, the Wampus Cat Queen was said to be especially vengeful toward misbehaving children. Many a lazy country boy had accomplished his chores with renewed enthusiasm when informed of the gruesome outcome of being cornered by the Queen.

Scores of children reported spotting the beast, but the only confirmed sighting was by Mayor Millard J. Underwood, of Bald Creek, Georgia on a cold night in January many years ago. The mayor was a sober man and Sunday School teacher. He had no bad habits and was known to have no perversions of any sort. On the night in question, the mayor's less reliable cousin, Floyd Atwater, accompanied Mayor Underwood as they trooped along the Cove Road after a spirited revival meeting at the Baptist Church. Floyd was keenly aware that the Queen considered the spongy livers of hard-drinking men to be a special delicacy. Without warning, a figure with the body of a mountain lion leapt out of the woods and onto the trail. The animal's hideous scream echoed through the ridges. The god-awful smell was worse than the terrifying noise. Floyd described the odor as that of a wet dog climbing out of a privy.

The men spun on their heels and hightailed it back to the church where a few people were still milling around. The mayor attested to every word of Floyd's story. As Floyd described his terror, his eyes bulged, he clutched his chest, keeled over, and died on the spot.

Try as they might, folks were unable to close poor Floyd's eyes in death. He was buried the next afternoon in a meadow near the Cove Road. Around midnight, people who lived along the stretch of road near Floyd's grave heard what they described as the blood-chilling squall of a deranged woman.

At daybreak a group of well-armed citizens approached the burial site. They found that dirt had been strewn over a wide area and Floyd's pine coffin ripped to shreds. There was neither hide nor hair of Floyd Atwater. The region smelled of rotten eggs and long-dead

8

vermin. People say the open grave is there today for anyone brave enough to go in search of it.

Then, there's the pitiful story of Arvil Ogleby. In the 1920's Arvil eked out a living on a rocky, hardscrabble farm near the head of Big Cat Cove. He lived hand-to-mouth with his strong-willed wife, nine unruly children, and a demented mother-in-law. One day just about sunset, Arvil whistled a tune and took a little stroll down the Cove Road.

He never returned!

No trace of Arvil Ogleby was ever found. Neighbors swore that the fiendish Wampus Cat had consumed a God-fearing man.

Folks all around the Cove spoke with sympathy about the fate of Arvil. But no one felt sorry when Baxter Davis turned up missing. Ol' Doc Weymer told the story of stopping at the Davis' shack on several occasions to tend to Baxter's battered wife. Then one day he was called to the home and was surprised when Thelma Davis met him on the porch having suffered no injuries.

"It's our oldest, Mary Beth. Her arm is broken. The girl's in agony."

Sure enough, the fourteen-year-old had a broken arm and severe bruising.

"How did this happen?"

"She fell off a horse. Ain't that right, honey?"

"Yes, Momma. That's right."

The physician set the arm and was preparing to leave when he looked around and asked, "Where's Baxter?"

Mrs. Davis dabbed her eyes with the helm of her apron. "Haven't you heard? Strangest thing. Baxter left us. Left his clothes, his gun, his dog, everything. He just walked off down the Cove Road and never came back. I bet anything the Wampus Cat Queen got him."

The doctor tossed his bag on the passenger seat of his car, and then he noticed a fertile patch of ground in the vegetable garden where tomato plants were already bursting through the soft earth.

"Would you look at that? Seems your tomatoes are doing real well, Thelma."

"Yes, doctor. We've had an early spring. Life is going to be better this year."

Word soon got around that the Wampus Cat Queen had claimed another victim.

***

Homer appeared courageous as they set out on schedule. Elwood made no pretense of confidence. Sweat poured down his forehead. His heart raced to the pace of his chattering teeth.

The trail was a gloomy tunnel into hell. About three miles along their trek, the woodlands thickened and crept closer to the road. The path disappeared into darkness too dim for the boys to see their feet. They groped along feeling with their toes the bends and turns of the narrow track. Elwood's jangled nerves generated an urgent need to empty his bladder, but he was reluctant to stand still even for a few seconds.

The light improved when they came to an open area with pasture on both sides of the road near the Tucker Farm.

"I gotta take a leak." Elwood fumbled with his zipper. Soon, the tension was flowing away. Elwood raised his head, looked around at the dimly lit fields, and listened to the chirping of crickets and the sound of splatter on the grass.

Elwood shook off a couple of droplets and took a long sigh.

"MURRARRA!"

The loudest, most terrifying, otherworldly sound imaginable pierced the night air. The earsplitting roar came from a source no more than thirty yards from where the boys stood. Elwood's heart thumped to a stop. He struggled to draw another breath and scanned the area for Homer. But Homer had vanished.

Elwood's heart restarted with the awful realization that he was alone within a few yards of god-knows-what. He reached for the tab on his zipper and gave it a firm jerk, forgetting to stow away. Intense pain rocked his tender nether region. He yowled, momentarily disregarding the baleful sound that prompted his error in procedure.

Then it came again, the dreadful squall of a dozen suffering souls. Elwood struggled vigorously to free himself from the carnivorous zipper. Then terror and dread shot though his body. *It was the Wampus Cat Queen. Sure as shit!*

There could be no doubt about the fate of Homer. Elwood shuddered to think that he would soon be joining his friend in the belly of a monster. His trembling increased the pelvic pangs of a thousand nerve endings.

Elwood looked heavenward. "God, this here's Elwood. It's Elwood Albert Hatmaker from Ludowici. That's in Georgia. I'm in one hell of a fix down here. The Wampus Cat Queen is gonna get me. And God, I can't even run. You see, junior is hung up real bad. He's caught in this damn zipper, and I can't get him loose. Looks like I'm gonna die right here soon as that Wampus Cat Queen sniffs me. God, if you do get me outta this mess, I'll go to Mount Harmony every Sunday. I won't ever think nasty about girls again. Tell Mamma not to grieve too much. Guess I'll be seeing you—soon."

***

Unbeknownst to Homer and Elwood, the saga of Charger played a fateful role in their misfortune and terror.

Charger was born on the farm of Elmer Tucker. His dad, Bob, was the most proficient bull to ever live on the farm. Charger's mother, Deloris, was stingy with her milk but an excellent reproducer.

When the rambunctious calf was three weeks old, he charged into a group of calves, sending them scurrying in all directions. Elmer Tucker watched the antics of his calf. "That's gonna be my new bull. I'm gonna call him Charger."

Thus, Charger avoided the fate of most male calves. Little did the other young males realize that their futures were about to be dealt a cruel blow. They would have suffered even greater consternation if they had known that the purpose of castration was to make muscles softer, and, alas, more chewable.

By the age of three, Charger was a fully mature bull and more than ready for his life's pursuit. Charger, a workaholic, performed his duties admirably when the cows came into estrus, what the farmers called "season." By mid April, Charger had impregnated every cow in his company.

When the final cow was no longer interested in socializing, Charger did not have much to do except eat, sleep, and look forward to the next spring.

April finally arrived. Charger was near the barn, munching on a bale of hay. His nose twitched. A faint, familiar scent wafted in the air. A couple of minutes later, another breeze filtered through the trees. This time the aroma was unmistakable—a cow in season!

Charger trotted to the far end of the field. His nose told him that he was heading in the right direction. A strong fence separated him from his objective. Built to confine a bull, the fence was not at all like the frail barriers surrounding the cows. But this was a big bull, and he was on a mission.

The fence consisted of two rows of parallel boards. The bottom plank was about two feet above the ground, the top plank another two feet higher. Charger banged his horns against the top section of lumber with no result. He backed up several feet and slammed into the top board. Again, the plank held fast.

Charger retreated twenty yards. He snorted and dug into the dirt with his fore hooves. A brisk gust of wind filled his flaring nostrils with an enticing scent. He charged, thrusting more than a ton of amorous intention against the top plank. The screws held tightly, but the board shattered. The longer section of the broken lumber hung down at a steep angle, no longer an obstacle to inflamed passion.

Charger triumphantly strode over the lower plank, preparing to advance into a pasture that was the parlor of the first cow to be in season. His belly slid across the rough bottom plank, embedding several long splinters deep into his flesh. Worst of all, the lumber removed a section of hide. Blood trickled, then poured from the wound. Searing pain shot through Charger's nervous system.

"MURRARRA!" He roared loud and long with a mixture of agony and the frustration of unfulfilled lust.

Charger backed off the lower board, re-scraping already damaged tissue. Horrendous bellowing reverberated through the trees.

Finally free, Charger glared at bits of red meat clinging to the plank. He would not attempt another crossing, no matter if a bouquet descended upon him from a bovine angel standing at heaven's gate.

***

Elwood concluded his prayer and tried once more to free himself from the man-eating zipper. He tugged vigorously and, perhaps with the help of God, Elwood's precious member snapped free.

"Praise the Lord. Oh, thank God."

With his most private part safely tucked inside his underwear, Elwood again pulled on the zipper. It would not budge. A bit of ragged flesh was wedged in the vicious metal teeth.

Elwood broke into an all-out sprint in spite of considerable pain intensified by the jostling of his loins. A mile passed in a few minutes. Elwood was on the verge of collapse.

Two hundred yards ahead of Elwood around the Cove Road, Homer heard something coming along the road behind him. It could be Elwood, or it could be the Queen. Homer was not about to hang around to find out. For the next three hours, Homer maintained a safe distance between himself and whoever or whatever was trailing him.

Elwood neared the safety of the head of Big Cat Cove. He stopped to catch his breath. For the second time that fateful night, Elwood lifted his eyes toward Heaven:

"God, this here's Elwood. It's Elwood Albert Hatmaker from Ludowici. Looks like I'm gonna make it. But Lord, I think the Queen got Homer. I ain't seen him. And he wouldn't leave me all by myself with junior tangled in that stupid zipper, and the Wampus Cat Queen about to eat me alive. Lord, this night you will welcome home the soul of Homer Guthry. God, listen to me. If that Wampus Cat didn't kill Homer, I'm gonna kill him myself."

WILSON'S DREAM

Life was almost perfect for Wilson, a hulking black and tan Coonhound. He romped through meadows and sniffed everything that required sniffing in the backwoods of Long County.

On a sweltering August day, Wilson was giving his nose a workout in a Georgia pine forest while his human companions, Homer Guthry and Elwood Hatmaker, played and swam in Blue Deep Hole.

Wilson looked up as Elwood strode into a thicket, making his way through a tangle of shrubs and briars. Red strawberries glistened against dark green leaves. Wild flowers blossomed in the blistering sun. The clean mountain air was infused with the fragrance of hundreds of honeysuckle blooms.

Wilson tilted his head to one side as Elwood reached deep into the hollow of a dead oak tree. Elwood's big grin spread from ear to ear. He held high a pint of moonshine in a Mason jar. "Let's split this here pint of Possum Pee."

Homer and Elwood kicked back in the shade of a giant maple tree.

The morning had been exhausting for Wilson. First, a squirrel made sure that Wilson caught sight of him before scampering onto a high limb. A rabbit got away after a circuitous chase.

Then Wilson suffered the exasperation of trying to get a turtle out of its shell. Wilson scratched and bit the shell with mounting frustration. After a couple of minutes, Wilson ambled away and stood with his rear toward the motionless reptile. The turtle's head snuck a tentative appearance. Wilson whirled and pounced. His teeth clamped nothing but air. The wary turtle was too clever and too quick to be foiled by a lumbering hound. Wilson affectionately licked the seam in the shell where the turtle's head had vanished. "Hey, let's be friends." The ruse didn't work, and Wilson abandoned all hope of turtle steak.

The shallow waters surrounding Blue Deep Hole teemed with nourishment. Wilson crept to the water's edge and hunched down to watch as tiny fish darted through the water. He knew that small fish were impossible to catch, but a big trout meandered in eight inches of water. Wilson stalked around the area until he stood between the trout and deeper water. With a headlong leap, Wilson landed with a resounding splash that sent up a spray of cold water. The startled fish swam quickly away from the commotion and into the rocky shallows. With its movement restricted, the trout was easy prey for the ravenous hunter. Wilson ripped open the fish's belly and gobbled up the soft innards.

Wilson ambled along with his nose to the ground. He trotted back and forth across the path, backtracking when he picked up the scent of a rabbit.

Wilson panted steadily as he sauntered over to where the boys were reclining in the shade. Homer took another swig as Elwood gave Wilson a few strokes along his rough back. "Good dog."

Wilson shuffled over to Homer where he received more kind words and comforting touches. Worn-out, he looked for a site to take a nap. Wilson turned in a figure eight before flopping onto his belly, keeping his head up with his forelegs tucked under him. He yawned, stretching his mouth and snapping it closed.

A minute later, Wilson glanced at his human friends. The boys snored and snorted. Lowering his chin to the ground between his front paws, Wilson closed his eyes. He began to dream:

It's springtime. A plump rabbit is far from his hole. Amanda, the neighbor's leggy French Poodle, digs from under her enclosure. She peers coyly from behind a bush.

Ahhh, Amanda.

Fluttering eyelashes hint of a frisky mood. A breeze confirms that the temptress is indeed feeling romantic. "Bonjour, Monsieur Wilson."

"How y'all doin', honey pot?"

"Oh Monsieur, I just love b-e-e-g country fellows. Come closer. Whisper amour in my ear."

With the regal bearing of a Great Dane, Wilson struts into the bushes where his paramour awaits. Amanda looks over her shoulder, swaying her arched tail with seductive twitches. Wilson rolls up his tongue. Then, he slings a mouthful of dirt from his teeth. He circles her with a single thought in mind.

Amanda abandons all pretense of modesty.

Wilson growls, "Amour, amour, here we go."

"Wake up, dog! Come on, wake up. We gotta be going."

Wilson opened one eye. His head cleared as the image of Amanda dissolved, replaced by the face of . . . Elwood.

"Oh no! Down, boy, don't bite me. Help! Somebody, help!"

THAT DOG WILL BITE YOU

No more than a few kids knew about the secret location of Blue Deep. Homer and Elwood met each day at the swimming hole deep in the pine forest along Coddler's Creek. Cold, greenish water spilled over algae-clad boulders and collected in an azure pond. Sunlight penetrated the surface and spawned streaks of violet. The pool was rumored to be bottomless.

A short board was tied to the end of a thirty-foot rope attached high in a cottonwood tree. The boys would swing out over the lake to a height of about fifteen feet before releasing the rope and yelling, "Geronimo!" Arms and legs flailed away as the guys tumbled buck-naked into the chilly water.

Elwood brought along a Beagle he called "Cat" for reasons known only to Elwood. Homer's dog, a Coonhound, had the more conventional name of Wilson.

The fun of swimming in Blue Deep and playing with their dogs was enhanced by the thrill of doing something forbidden.

Homer and Elwood had a taste for moonshine. The local distributor of untaxed spirits, Lefty Goins, would not dream of giving booze to the youngsters. Lefty had a reputation to uphold. In fact, Lefty's scruples were unassailable, except where money was involved. He allowed the boys to purchase slush from the bottom of the cooker mixed with the good stuff that he called Possum Pee. Lefty often hid a Ball jar half full of liquor in the hollow of a dead stump about fifty yards in back of his drinking establishment, the Tattletale Roadhouse & Social Club. The boys had their hands on the first pint they had gotten in more than a month. The temperature neared ninety-five degrees as they lounged on the edge of Blue Deep. Homer was tipsy. Elwood, about one swallow from zonked. Homer and Elwood wore silly grins and watched as their dogs romped on the bare ground.

Wilson began to stretch and yawn. The hound reached forward with his front paws and pushed back on his haunches until his chest almost touched the ground. He circled to his left a couple of times and flopped down on his right side. Wilson raised his left hind leg, hiking it high above his head. Then he tenderly licked his scrotum.

Homer observed the dog's contortion with amazement. "Boy, I wish I could do that."

Elwood yelled, "Are you crazy? That dog will bite you! Oh, God, I can't watch."

LIKE YOU NEVER HEARD

Homer Guthry and Elwood Hatmaker had been friends since boyhood. All grown up, they sipped moonshine on a Saturday night at the Tattletale Roadhouse & Social Club, a backwoods establishment that featured a locally processed beverage known as Possum Pee.

Homer and Elwood began the evening slowly, but were soon consuming the 100-proof hooch as if it were cider. Around midnight, Homer noticed that the floor had a definite slant. He pleaded with Elwood to help him hold the table before the whole joint slid against the west wall.

Homer was ready to go home. He pulled himself to his feet and clasped a half-full jar of Possum Pee with both hands. He climbed across the steep floor, pushed up through the door, and stumbled into the cold night air. He pulled up his collar as snowflakes shimmered in the moonlight and whirled to a wintery waltz.

He dreaded the mile-and-a-quarter walk home. The path wound through creepy woods and around a swamp teeming with fearsome creatures. He worried about stepping on a rattlesnake or copperhead in the dark.

Homer took a deep draw from his Ball jar and sat out on his perilous trek. He staggered through a gloomy stretch where pine trees clustered on both sides of the narrow road. Clouds blocked most of the light from the moon. Spanish moss hung from branches and swung to and fro in a ripe breeze. An owl whoo-whooed a warning.

Halfway into the thicket, the level road tilted to the left and then to the right. Homer fell to his knees with the infernal swaying. A minute later, the road leveled out a bit, and Homer got to his feet. Then, out of the gloom came a commanding voice.

"Homer."

"Say what?"

Nothing. Not a whisper. Homer swallowed hard.

"Homer."

"I heard you. Who's there?"

Homer tried to detect any movement in the undergrowth. The wind picked up, but he couldn't see anything unusual.

"Homer, this is God."

"Yeah, r-r-right. You're a sumbitch trying to scare me. I see you, and I got a gun." Homer searched frantically for his broken-bladed pocketknife.

"This is thy God."

"I ain't buying that crap. You better show yourself right now."

There was a moment of agonizing silence as Homer trembled. A pint of cold sweat rolled down his body.

"Know that I am God."

This time the voice boomed from directly overhead, and Homer became convinced he was indeed talking to God. "Sorry. Real damn sorry. I didn't recognize you. What I'm saying is that I didn't know it was you."

"I want you to spread my word."

"Yeah, sure, but there's been some mistake. No, wait, I didn't mean that, exactly. Well sort of. I mean you got the wrong Homer. I'm Homer Guthry. I'm Maude Amy's oldest boy."

"Yes, I know."

Homer wanted nothing to do with sober, moral living. "I can't spread nobody's word. I ain't got no learning. I can't spell shi— sugar."

Homer took another swig from his jar. "Thou, I mean Thee, got to knowest I ain't a good guy. I'm awful bad to drink. I drink Possum Pee. I mean juice. I drink possum juice. I swear like a sailor, and I don't bathe up on a regular basis. You can ask anybody. I'm saying I ain't your man. I think about girls all the time. You know what I'm talkin' about. Bare-butt-naked girls. I even dream about 'em. You wouldn't believe the nasty in my dreams. Oh hell, I shouldn't be telling you this stuff. I'm nervous as a hog passing peach seeds. W-a-i-t, wait, wait! I didn't mean to say nothing like that. God knows—I mean Ye knows I ain't worth killin'. Oh Lord, I didn't mean that neither. Hell—oh damn it, I mean heck."

Homer lowered his head and mumbled, "Shit, I can't get nothing right."

Homer made one more attempt to persuade God that Maude Amy's oldest boy should not be selected for any worthwhile purpose.

"Ye, er, Thou knowest I ain't no good to nobody for nothing. It's a fact. I'm one sorry bastard. You can ask anybody up and down this god—uh , up and down this here hollow. They'll tell you I ain't worth powder and a bullet."

"Take not my name in vain."

"Oh, hell no. I wouldn't do that. I'm sure of it. I swear sumpin' awful, but I wouldn't do nothing like that, ever."

An eerie light spread from somewhere deep in the woods. Black iron gates materialized and slowly begin to creak open. Homer's teeth clattered with the bobbing of his head.

The gates sprang open! Homer screamed like a panther. A gust of white-hot heat nearly fried his bulging eyeballs. Fire engulfed the woods amid the agonizing groans of suffering souls. Homer's greatest terror was the snakes, thousands of them, all slithering and flicking out their dreadful tongues, red eyes glowing like coals of fire.

Homer fainted and collapsed face-down in the dirt.

He awoke when the sun came up the next morning. His head throbbed as he got to his knees. Homer gazed heavenward. "God, this here's Homer Guthry. I'll do any damn thing you want. I hadn't counted on them snakes being, you know, down there. I ain't ever gonna think nasty about girls again except for Susie Baker—and her mother. Look for a red shirt on the third row. I'm gonna twitch around more than any of 'em, and sing like you never heard."

THE TATTLETALE ROADHOUSE & SOCIAL CLUB

The moonshine that Lefty Goins brewed deep in the woods behind his establishment, the Tattletale Roadhouse & Social Club, was known as Possum Pee. The booze was a clear liquid with the aroma of pine tar and a trace of brown-red residue from the rusty pipes of the still.

Bluford Nodding refused to drink a drop of Possum Pee or any other alcohol. He had wanted to be a Baptist preacher, but a learning disability prevented him from obtaining even an elementary school education. Exclusion from the mainstream ministry was a bitter disappointment to Bluford, but it had not dented his determination to be of service to the Lord. He went all over town preaching about the evils of strong drink. From a safe distance, children would taunt the one-man temperance union and local legend:

There's Bluford Nodding, big and strong
A man of God who does no wrong
It is true, of the devil's brew
Not a sip gets passed his lips

From time to time Bluford would burst into the Tattletale, tattered old Bible in hand, looking for souls to save from liquor. Lefty would have thrown the intruder out on his rear, but Bluford was a towering, muscular man, and not opposed to dispensing righteous wrath upon anyone interfering with God's work. Not a man in the Long County was willing to take on Bluford Nodding.

One cool autumn evening, Bluford limped into the Tattletale with a walking cane in his right hand.

"What's matter, Bluford?"

"The devil's put a terrible curse on me. They call it the gout, but like Job of old, I got the strength to fend off a dozen demons."

Bluford dropped his backside down with a flop that almost

25

collapsed a chair. The tavern was bustling with twelve sinners, including four daughters-of-Satan sipping moonshine from Ball jars and sharing a spittoon, but evangelism would have to wait until Bluford could find relief from his god-awful suffering.

Lefty watched Bluford tenderly touch the swollen big toe on his right foot. A light went on in the moonshiner's head. This was his chance to collect on a bet that he could never get a dribble of Possum Pee into Bluford Nodding. Lefty disappeared into the back room for a couple of minutes and emerged with a bottle of Doctor Quick's Liniment. The label boasted that the medication was an effective cure for all ailments and could be applied to the skin, or drunk straight from the bottle for the treatment of internal disorders. The elixir was an especially potent remedy for both constipation and diarrhea.

"Bluford, I got just what you need. This here concoction is heaven-sent. Poppa used it all the time for the thing that's ailing you. What did you call it?"

"It's the dad-burned gout."

"That's right. He used it for gout. It had him feeling like a red-headed schoolboy in no time."

Bluford accepted the bottle and examined it. "Did you daddy put this stuff on his toes or did he drink it?"

"Oh, he drank it. Poppa said the liquid gets in your joints. It's sort of like putting oil on a rusty hinge."

Bluford held the foul-smelling medication to his nose. Then a shooting pain ripped through his toe. "Oh Lord, my toe's a coming off." He removed the cork and gulped three ounces. His eyes bulged. He clawed his sizzling belly. "My stomach's tryin' to crawl outta my butt."

The pain in his right foot took second place to the inferno in his gut. "I'm dying! God is calling me home. Everybody stand back. My chariot's comin' through that door."

"Take it easy, Bluford. You'll feel better in a minute."

Sure enough, the fire in his tummy subsided, along with the pain in his foot. Bluford swished another ounce of liniment between his teeth and swallowed hard.

"My throat's on fire, but hey, I feel all warm and fuzzy, and my foot don't hurt so much. My joints are looser than a goose in a green apple patch."

Lefty refilled the bottle from a supply in the back room. Almost half a pint later, the would-be preacher wore a goofy grin and an air of supreme confidence. He sat back and looked around as the floor swayed to the rhythms of Eddie Arnold.

Bluford noticed that old lady Ellen Eldridge possessed the most appealing eyes and a bountiful bosom. Gravity had taken a toll on Ellen's heavy breasts, but to Bluford they were as firm as spring melons. Bluford had never so much as kissed a girl, but pent-up hormones spurted like a broken water pipe. Rampaging testosterone dredged up the primal urges of a bull moose. His nostrils flared as he stalked Ellen with the focus on a hawk staring at a blind rabbit.

On unsteady legs, and clutching his cane, Bluford approached Ellen with a gleam in his bleary eyes. He tilted his head and cocked an eyebrow. "Hey, hey, hey, little lady."

Ellen put down her jar. With a shy smile and fluttering eyelashes, she looked up at the tipsy giant. Bluford pushed his capacity to be debonair to the limit. "You know, you're pretty foxy for an old broad."

"Why, Bluford, I didn't know you knew how to say sweet things."

"Yeah, I got some smarts people don't know 'bout."

"Bluford Nodding, if I didn't know better, I would think that you're under the influence of alcohol."

"I ain't under no alfluence of inkehol."

Ellen was determined not to let this opportunity pass. It had been ages since any man had shown an interest in her, much less a strapping young man six-and-a half feet tall with huge hands. She glanced at Bluford's bulging biceps and tight jeans. Bluford Nodding was going to get lucky.

"Bluford, I believe you have intentions toward me."

"Naw, Ellen, it ain't nothing like that. I just want to get in your britches."

Ellen tried to be coy, the same way she had been many years ago as a voluptuous young woman. She murmured under her breath. "Men don't want nookie to be too easy. Guys are funny that way."

Ellen described a test Bluford would have to pass before he could enjoy her charms. "First, you have to name all the states that begin with the letter 'M'."

Bluford thought for a second. "Let's see, there's Mimmissippi, Mimmesota, and oh yeah, Mimmouri. That's it."

Tony R. Lindsay

"Bluford Nodding, you should be ashamed of yourself. You missed Montana, Maryland, Michigan, Maine, and Massachusetts."

"You missed one too, Ellen. You missed Mexico."

Ellen took another look at Bluford's massive hands and oversized feet. "Tell you what, Bluford. You name just one state that borders on an ocean, and we're gonna get on that couch in Lefty's back room, and I'm gonna make you glad you're a man."

Bluford's heart pounded. He racked his brain. "I got it. How about Kentucky?"

Ellen took Bluford by the hand. "Close enough."

FORGET MY SOUL

Bluford Nodding, a dim-witted, towering sequoia of a man, carried his Bible and mumbled a prayer as he plodded along a path deep in the woods. Bluford neared Okefenokee Swamp, careful to avoid quicksand pits pocking the soft ground. A puff of air assaulted his nostrils with the stench of rotting vegetation. Misty fog reflected diffused light filtering through the trees. Dragonflies and mosquitoes hovered and darted like tiny biplanes in a Lilliputian world. Ancient live oaks, elegant as spiral staircases, swaggered in the wind above less noble trees.

"Help! For God's sake, help me."

The hoarse shout came from behind a stand of cyprus trees. Bluford edged along a narrow ridge, pushing aside low-hanging Spanish moss. He discovered a scrawny man up to his knees in the black water of the bog. A camouflage hat covered with fishing lures floated in the muck.

"Oh, thank God. I can't move my feet. You got to get me out of this shit."

Bluford clutched his Bible to his chest and covered it with huge hands to protect the holy book from the angry words streaming from the stranger's mouth. "You ort not be talkin' like that."

"Forget it. Pull me out of here. This stupid swamp is about to swallow my ass."

"Ain't no cause to swear. It's a sin and you ort ta be 'shamed. Ain't never heard a man callin' on God and swearing sumpin' fierce all at the same time."

"Look, numbnuts, I don't have time for a sermon from the likes of you. Pull me out of here before it's too late."

"Ain't doin' nuttin fer you 'til I hears you pray the way the Laard done learned us to pray."

Bluford turned to leave.

"Oh crap! Don't go. I'll pray right now. Listen to me. Our Father who art in heaven, hollowed be Thy name. Thy kingdom come, Thy will be . . . ."

"Wait, wait, wait. Hold it right thar. That ain't right."

"It's The Lord's Prayer, for heaven's sake. Don't tell me it's not

29

right."

"You ain't a prayin' proper. You ain't in the right spirit. God done told me not ta help you lessen you prays with a sweet voice good 'nuff for His ears without no swearin'."

"Ugahhh! This damn sludge is up to my chest. You stupid sumbitch, help me."

"I'm gonna ask God to forgive your soul for them words a spewin' forth out of your dark heart."

"Forget my soul. Save my ass!"

Bluford looked toward the sky. He held his Bible high. "Laard, this here's Bluford. It's Bluford Nodding, Laard. Now we done ask that you forgive . . ."

"Get on with it. Hurry up, fool."

"Don't you city fellers know not to interrupt a man when he's a talkin' to the Laard. Ain't you got no kind of smarts? Hush up while I calls on God."

"Yeah, okay, just hurry, please hurry."

"Laard, this here's Bluford. It's Bluford Nodd . . ."

"Stupid idiot. Listen to me, Bluford. God knows it's you. Mother Mary knows it's you. Peter and Paul and all the saints, they know it's you. The fuckin' devil knows it's you!"

"Laard, this here's Bluford. It's Bluford Nodding, Laard. This here fisherman feller done walked right into . . ."

"Ugahhh-Ugahhh. I can't stand it. I'd rather die than hear you say "Laard" one more time. No, wait. I didn't mean that."

"Laard, this here fisherman done walked right into the swamp. He ain't got a lick of sense, and he ain't a bit nice. Reckon you'll be dealing with his soul right soon. And now, Laard, I ask You to comfort them that's done sick and them folks that's done afflicted in this here holler. And Laard . . ."

"Forget the damn sickies. Forget the afflicted bastards. Save my ass!"

"There y'all go swearin' even when your eyes done be bulgin' like eggs from a chicken's butt."

Brackish water washed over the fisherman's neck. Putrid sludge seeped into the corners of his mouth. Tears streamed down his cheeks. "God, oh, dear God, I don't want to die." He took a deep breath and held it.

Bluford bent a strong sapling until the branches were within the man's grasp.

"Now that thar's a proper prayer, young feller."

MUD DUCK AND NIMROD

Mud Duck Morris shouted over the din in the Tattletale Roadhouse & Social Club. "Every damn thing I like is illegal, immoral, or fattening."

"Yeah, man, I know what you mean," responded his hard-drinking friend, Nimrod Keller.

"Hey, Billy Ray, get me another mug a beer will ya? Get Nim one, too."

"Sure, Mud Duck, who's countin'?"

"Like I was saying, Nim, I can't have any fun except when I am with my sweet Anna Belle."

"Why not?"

"I never get what I really want from other girls. They are always squeaking, 'I just want to be your friend.' Hell, I don't need another damn friend."

"Yeah, I hear that a lot," sighed Nimrod.

"Even Mom doesn't understand me. She knows I have a bent toward racy srories, so for my birthday she got me a subscription to *Cosmopolitan*. She says they have a lot of really hot articles like 'Thirty-one Ways to Make Your Lover Happy as Hell.' Crap like that. What I really wanted was a subscription to *Tomcat's Legal Lovelies*."

"Mud, I just got the new issue. Did you see that Vickie from Melbourne? That's in Australia. Holy moly, what a doll. Kinda makes a feller want to find a way to get down there—uh, to Australia, I mean."

Nimrod reached into his hip pocket and pulled out a page torn from the magazine. He slipped Vickie's photo into Mud Duck's lap.

"Yeah, Nim, she's a beauty. Buck-naked, and smiling like she's singing in the choir on Sunday morning. It's just a guess, but I bet she ain't shy when it comes to humpin'."

Nimrod and Mud Duck savored gulps of beer and licked their lips. Mud Duck looked deep into the amber liquid. "And another thing, Nim. You know I got a tendency toward corpulence."

"Oh, my God!"

"It means fat, stupid."

"Oh."

"Mom says I'm too chunky. She says I got to consume less and exercise more. I hate exercise. It wears me out. And I need the nourishment that I get from drinking. When it comes to liquor, I like Possum Pee. They don't pay tax on that stuff, and it tastes better than the store-bought kind. Works better, too. Anna Belle likes it a lot. She's my kind of girl."

"Yeah, all the guys like Anna Belle. I hear she bangs like a screen door."

"Hey, don't be talking 'bout Anna Belle."

"Relax, Mud. All I'm saying is that she ain't real pretty, but she's got a generous nature."

"Listen, Nim. Anna Belle is special to me. We have a relationship. Something you wouldn't understand."

"Guess not."

Mud Duck nears the bottom of his pint. "Yeah, Anna Belle is the cerebral type."

"Funny, I never would have thought that about her."

"It means she's smart, dumb-ass."

"Oh."

"She's smart, and a sweet person with a big heart. She's got four old dogs and a blind cat. I keep her three-legged fox at my place."

Neither man spoke for a moment as they drained their brews.

"Say, Mud, you gonna marry Anna Belle?"

"A fellow could do a lot worse. A guy like me could marry some skinny beauty queen who thinks about nothing but her precious self. Bloodhounds like you would be on her trail all the time. Anna Belle is different. She can laugh at herself and she hardly ever gets mad. When she laughs, folks around her chuckle even though they don't know what she's howling 'bout. Anna Belle doesn't hold back. She wrings every ounce of good feeling out of a laugh. I love everything about her."

Nimrod searched for a spider that had disappeared under the rim of the bar as Mud Duck continued. "Anna Belle's got big bones and more curves than a cue ball. She's built for comfort, like a Cadillac. You know, warm and cozy on a cold winter night."

"Yeah, but them summer nights are gonna get sticky."

"Nimrod Keller, you don't have the brains of a tulip. I don't know why I talk to you about affairs of the heart. You ain't nothing but a bucket of lust." Mud Duck gazed into the distance. "With me, it's all about love. Anna Belle, my sweet Anna Belle."

"Yeah, and she's got a big ass."

"You little weasel. What did you say?"

"Uh, I said… Jordache. She wears Jordache."

"What you don't understand, nitwit, is that love is as soft as a sigh."

"Yeah, soft like a virgin's thigh."

"Nim, there's no hope for you. You're as low as whale manure."

"I guess I ain't the celibate type."

"What you're trying to say is 'cerebral'."

"I ain't that neither. I just want to move to Australia and settle down in a cabin in the middle of the Outback. All by ourselves, me and Vicky, and forty kegs of beer."

HAWKSHAW HAWKS AND HOG ALBRIGHT

Lefty Goins shook his head as he slid a Ball jar along the bar. "Horniest fellows I ever did see. Those two galoots are still looking for the crack of dawn. Hawkshaw smells like a wet turtle climbing out of a privy, and Hog is the only rascal I ever heard tell of who gets a kick out of blowing bubbles in a mud puddle."

Hawkshaw Hawks and Hog Albright were the scum of Long County. The lying, thieving, lowlife scoundrels loved to drink moonshine known to all as Possum Pee. And they were crazy about women. It didn't matter what a lass looked like. Hawkshaw and Hog were eager for some loving from the lowest-hanging fruit in all of Georgia. When fanned by a dose of Possum Pee, their natural state of readiness ignited into an inferno of passion.

Females, young and old, whispered stories about Hawkshaw and Hog, but few were willing to spend a minute in the company of a despicable weasel and a slow-witted oaf.

However, the DiGiornio Sisters, Fellasha and Insaysha, were unlike any other women.

The buxom twins possessed four breasts exceeding the combined mammary tissue of the soprano section of the Mormon Tabernacle Choir. Their phenomenal lust was matched by their ravenous appetite for groceries.

Hawkshaw and Hog were lushed the night they staggered out of the Tattletale and were pounced on by the DiGiornio sisters. An orgy ensued at Hog's place beyond the likes of the finest brothel of ancient Rome. Three giant bodies heaved and pulsated. Bone-skinny Hawkshaw bounced around like a mouse cavorting atop a trio of hippos.

In the midst of the group grope, Hawkshaw had an idea. "Why don't we's all get married? We could have ourselves a double ceremony."

The romantic notion overwhelmed the lovely Insaysha. "Daddy's gonna be so proud." Her tears added to the pool of sweat covering the worn carpet.

Tony R. Lindsay

Soon afterward, Reverend Homer Guthry presided over a ribald wedding celebration on the lawn of the Tattletale Roadhouse and Social Club. Shady Mildew & his Happy Clappers Band hammered out an ear-splitting rendition of "Haystack Hannah."

The dregs of Long County society soaked up unimaginable decadence. Slither Reed lined up models of both sexes for his devoted interest in photographic anatomy. Ha-Ha-He-He Rhodes managed a rare half-smile while posing with his friend for one of Slither's action shots. The father of the brides sobbed in the affectionate embrace of Willy Stover. Sweaty Betty Hatfield left a trail like a snail. Lonnie Mae Wilcox was a young thing and the most innocent female at the gala event. "If this party gets any rougher," she said, "I'm gonna put my clothes on and go home."

The randy foursome settled down in a dilapidated farmhouse near Ludowici. Hawkshaw and Hog got jobs working side by side in the slaughterhouse. The girls were unable to find work, and lounged around consuming stale bread and wilting vegetables from the Farmer's Benevolent Society, and sides of beef stolen from the slaughterhouse.

Life became boring. Hawkshaw and Hog came home late every evening reeking with the stench of the slaughterhouse, dried blood under their fingernails, and loaded to their eyeballs with Possum Pee.

One Friday night, the sisters looked out the living room window to see their husbands crawling toward the front porch. Sick of the drunken louts, the girls bolted the door. When Hawkshaw and Hog realized they were locked out, they unscrewed the lid on one more pint of Possum Pee and soon lapsed into shallow comas.

Fellasha and Insaysha marched onto the porch and gazed down at the two soaked scalawags. Disgust became coldhearted vengeance. The twins used a wheelbarrow to move the boozehounds about eighty yards into a pine forest, and dumped them down a steep ravine. Two limp bodies tumbled and slid fifty feet into a marshy thicket.

Hours later, sunlight filtered through the trees. Hawkshaw roused Hog. "Wake up. Damn your ass anyway. Where the hell are we?"

"Dunno, cuz. Maybe we ain't in Georgia no more. Maybe we gonna die."

"Hog, there's only one thing we can do."

"Right on. Ain't but one thing for sure. Uh, what's that,

Hawkshaw?"

"We gotta pray."

"You ain't serious. I ain't never prayed before. Got no idea how it's done."

"Listen up, Hog. I heard Momma pray one time. She asked the Lord to strike Pa and the Widow Murphy dead so she wouldn't have to kill 'em. I figure we can ask where we're at and how we get home."

"But, Hawkshaw, God ain't gonna answer no prayer from the likes of us. The damn devil wouldn't listen to us."

"Stupid, you think I ain't thought 'bout that? I'm gonna disguise my voice so I sound like a city feller. You just keep quiet, don't belch or nothing."

"Right. You pray, and I'll be extra stilly. The Lord will think you're a sumbitch all by his lonesome."

Hawkshaw folded his hands under his chin, closed his eyes, and tilted his head toward heaven. "Lord, we need your help mighty bad down here. We're done lost."

Hawkshaw opened one eye and looked around. He cupped his right hand behind his ear, but there was no response from above.

He cleared his throat and raised his voice. "Lord, this here's Hawkshaw Hawks and Hog Albright, and we're lost bigger'n shit."

Hog bellowed, "Now you've done it. You done let God know it's us!"

MELANIE BURBER'S CHRISTMAS LETTER

Dear Friends and Family,

Melanie Burber here with an update of your favorite family. Bet y'all can't wait to learn what the Burber clan has been up to during the past year.

Me and Paul renewed our wedding vows last January. He'd been gone for such a long time, and we had missed his smiling face and financial support. Paul's a charmer, and he's done stole the hearts of our little ones, Billy, age three, and little Melissa, ten months.

Paul's really matured. Like he says, "Fourteen years in solitary confinement gives a feller time to think 'bout what's important in life."

Paul always had a way with words.

Can you believe our Randy will be nineteen this year? Where does time go? Randy's turned his life around. The Work-Release program is a wonderful experience for a boy who never held a job for more than a few days.

Randy's a darling boy, but they won't give him a Chinaman's chance. They had him up on some phony drug charges. The judge called Randy a low-level, bottom-feeding, no-account, scumbag middleman. As I understand it, a middleman buys and sells drugs. *And my boy ain't never sold a drug in his life!* Stupid-ass judge don't know shit.

They make Randy wear one of them fancy electronic devices around his left ankle. It makes him irritable as a scalded cat.

Randy had himself a nasty parole officer. They got into a terrible fistfight. She said he hit her first, but I saw the whole thing, and Randy didn't start it. Anyway, his attorney said, seeing as I'm Randy's mom, the dumb damn judge won't let me testify. Can you believe it? The boy's own mother can't tell them bastards what they need to know. Then the nitwit lawyer said something about the penal code. I'll tell you what I say: I say the damn penis system in this country is lousy!

We're all going to be praying for my baby on the sixteenth of next month when them highfalutin charlatans try to revoke his parole.

Randy is tall, strong, left-handed, and red headed. He's the spitting image of my brother, Marvin. It's a shame how people talk. You know that?

Hey, that's 'nuff about Randy. The pride and joy of the whole Burber family is our daughter, Eloise. She's sooo good-looking. Our neighbors say she looks like me—only better—much better. Her boyfriend said, when he first laid eyes on her he felt like a dog surrounded by four trees and not a leg to stand on. I mean, where do you look first?

Can y'all believe a Burber graduated from college? Eloise received a BA degree from The University of Georgia majoring in Everyday English. She wrote a poem about Christmas that tickled me.

Park the sleigh on the roof. Give the reindeer a break.
I have a present you'll be happy to take.

We'll turn the lights low. The bar will be stocked.
Forget the cold chimney, the door's unlocked.

This creature will stir you. At love I'm prolific:
You'll be moaning, "That was terrific!"

If you're exhausted and feeling tense,
You should get to know me in the biblical sense.

Soft music we'll play. Not a note of harsh Rap.
And when you're ready, I'll sit on your lap.

Very merry you'll be, on sheets of pure silk.
Unless you would rather have cookies and milk.

Ain't that precious? Eloise had a minor in Performing Arts. She moved to Los Angeles and hired herself an agent, Max Stone. He said that with Eloise's good looks and awesome talent, he would have her working in no time. Boy, he was right. She landed a job right away with High Rise Productions. *Can y'all believe she made seven movies in seven days?*

Eloise said she's working with three male stars that are really *b-i-i-g*. Our little Eloise, working with big stars. Oh, it just don't seem possible.

Her new best friend is a girl named Lotta Porsche. I guess she's from France or one of them places. Eloise said Lotta is the *sweetest* girl.

Max Stone told Eloise she ought to change her name. He said "Eloise Burber" just don't sound right.

Ta, Ta-Da… Ta, Ta-Daaaa…. Introducing, Miss Venus Mound.

Paul ain't happy. He's so proud of the Burber name.

I have to wind up this letter and get busy. I've already missed the bake sale down at Mount Harmony. This place is a mess and the dogs are running wild. Some days I just can't get myself going, especially when something is worrying me. And it's always something with Randy. I sent him to the store for cigarettes and vodka and he ain't come back.

And that was yesterday.

HAVE A GREAT YEAR
Melanie, Paul, Randy, Venus (Eloise), Billy, and little Melissa.

WILMA

Folks who don't believe in ghosts have never spent a night alone in a cemetery. Those of us with an open mind know the spirit world is a gospel fact. And it's not only the restless souls of our ancestors lurking in the dark. Any mountain man living in the backwoods of Georgia will tell you that bears leave ghosts behind upon passing from this life as surely as human ghosts haunt the sites of murders, hangings, and the empty homes of long-dead widows.

Silas Craven lived in the deep woods of Long County. Connoisseurs knew he produced the world's finest ninety-proof moonshine. Silas would tell anybody who would listen, "Them thar revenuers that want to keep a man from earnin' a honest livin' with nature's corn better give their hearts to God, 'cause their asses is mine. And I don't countenance them bears. They eat my makings."

The bootlegger was guarding his still on a cool, moonlit night in late October, his vigilant bear dog at his side. Wilma was descended from a long line of huge black-and-gray hounds especially bred to hunt bears.

Silas sat on the ground and pulled his collar high against his neck. Leaves covered his boots and piled against his shins. The stars in the night sky appeared to be proud of themselves.

A swig from his jar confirmed that the latest batch was up to standard. It lit a liquid fire going down his gullet and improved his perception of the world of Long County. Dog and man settled down for a little snooze.

Wilma began to snore softly. Bubbles oozed from her moist nose. From the depth of her consciousness, a foggy image became a suave, sleek, black Labrador. Wilma was coy, but she admired the stranger's confidence and dedication to the task at hand. The rhythm of her snoring was interrupted by a guttural utterance between a growl and a groan.

Meanwhile, Silas's eyes darted back and forth behind closed lids. A silly grin spread across his face. Then his eyes popped wide open, his dream of the Widow Murphy forgotten in an instant. *Somebody or something was out there!*

Silas knew that moonshine sharpens night vision. He took

another gulp and tried to focus on a dense patch of undergrowth. A faint blue light stirred in the gloom.

"Get the hell up, Wilma! Don't you see it? It's a bear or a damn revenuer. Go get him, girl."

Wilma bolted upright and snarled viciously. She turned in circles, unsure of the direction toward which she was supposed to launch her attack.

Silas stared into the blue haze. "There, you dumb shit. It's a goldarn bear."

Now dogs are smart, but they don't know the first thing about ghosts. Dogs can't see a ghost that's as plain as a water dish. And it's a rare dog that has a taste for whiskey.

The moonshiner pointed toward the bushes, but Wilma gazed at the tip of Silas' finger.

"You four-legged asshole. You ain't got no sense at all. Can't you smell the beast?"

Wilma tilted her head to one side.

"You yellow-livered lap dog, you ain't fit for nuttin'. You're a piss-poor excuse for a bear dog. A day-old goose got more sense than you. You lazy-ass, pussycat coward. Do I have to show you what to do?"

Wilma spun round and round in anticipation of something happening.

Silas got down on his hands and knees and sniffed the ground. "See that, goofball? Now sniff him out, sumbitch."

Wilma put her nose to the ground and sniffed mightily. Then looked up as if to say, "How's that, boss?"

"You worthless flea-bitten bag of chicken manure. At least you could bark. Would that be too much to ask of your majesty?"

Wilma bounced on her hind legs. Her front legs pawed the air.

"Your mother, Eunice, now there was a real bear dog. She warn't scared of nuttin'. She's in heaven, and I hope to hell she's lookin' the other way. She'd be ashamed of your ass, I can tell you that."

Silas jutted his blood-red face an inch from Wilma's nose. "Dumb-ass mongrel whore!"

Wilma got so excited she toppled over backwards.

Silas stomped the ground and slung his pipe into the woods.

At last, the hound got the idea she was supposed to be on the trail of something.

A huge bear with a bluish hue began to take shape. Silas downed a mouthful of moonshine. "There it is!"

Wilma picked up on the tone of Silas' voice and began an earnest search.

"Wilma, you idiot, you're trottin' right into that hairy bastard. Do sumpin' or you're gonna be joinin' ol' Eunice quicker'n shit."

The bear grinned as Wilma walked right through it. Silas clutched his chest. "Oh, Lord, it's a ghost bear!"

Silas tore through the forest like a terrified fox, his sphincter porous as a fish net.

He held the seat of his pants with both hands. "I'd kill you, Wilma. But you ain't worth a bullet."

Wilma bounded along joyously, her long tongue waving in the wind.

CLYDE

Life was in the dumper for Antonio Dioli. "I couldn't sell mosquito repellent to a caribou." The summer sales trip to Georgia from his home in Philadelphia had been a disaster. If his sales numbers didn't improve, he could forget about a year-end bonus.

That morning, Antonio's first wife had demanded an increase in alimony payments. She reminded him again that the kids needed braces.

Antonio had a red-hot prospect thirty miles from Savannah, but he had to arrive ahead of the competition. Time was running out to make his first sale in more than a week. Antonio's Chevrolet skidded to a stop in front of Clyde's Food and Stuff in Ludowici. He left the motor running and the air conditioner pumping cold air. The car's temperature gauge began a steady crawl.

The balding, rotund, forty-something salesman dashed into the store. Snapping up a package of TUMS, Antonio headed for the checkout counter, relieved to see no queue of customers.

A skinny clerk in his mid-fifties with "Clyde" scribbled in black ink on his white apron flashed a big smile. "How-da, young feller."

"Hello."

"That's some mighty nice weather we're having out there now, ain't it?"

"Yeah, sure."

"You want to know what my daddy alaze said?"

"No. I don't give a damn what your daddy *alaze said*."

"Daddy would look out the window at the bright sky, and he'd say, 'It looks so good out, *I think I'll leave it out.*' Daddy alaze said that. He did. Oh, Lardy. I swear he did. 'I think I'll leave it out.' Ol' Daddy was a card. He alaze . . ."

"Jeez Louise, can we move along here? I'm in a hurry."

Clyde withdrew a red handkerchief from his hip pocket and wiped tears from his eyes. "You one of them thar Yankee fellers, ain't ye?"

"That's right."

"What part of Yankee-land you from?"

"You probably never heard of it. It's called Philadelphia."

"You gonna love it down here, Mr. Yankee. The girls talk real slow. By the time a Southern girl says 'No' *it's too late*! Oh, Lardy, it's too late. You understand my meaning?"

"I understand your meaning. I'm not stupid you know."

"I thought I'd splain it to you. You being a Yankee and all."

"I'll have you know I graduated from Penn State."

"Lardy be. Ain't that sumpin'? I'm a graduate man myself. Clyde Pollard, Oak Grove Middle, Class of '52."

"Ignoramus. I'm smarter than any redneck."

"Lardy be. I heard tell that they are some smart Yankees. Ain't never met one though."

"Hurry, damn you."

"I knowed you's in a hurry. Lots of folks in a hurry these days. It's a shame, you know that?"

"Inbred hayseed. All the DNA is the same in Georgia. I told you to hurry."

"Okay. You just want one pack of them thar TUMS?"

Antonio's face turned purple. Veins on his neck bulged.

Clyde didn't notice the potential heart attack happening right in front of him. "Uncle Octavos—we call him Ott—he's a right smart pharmacy feller over in Peach Pit Hollar. Well, he says ya warn't be needin' no TUMS fer acid gestation if'n there warn't no tension. Yes, siree, tension can give you all sorts of ailments. Can even kill a feller if'n he ain't careful. You know what they say? Oh, by the way, did you ever wonder who 'they' is, anyway?"

"No! I don't give a rat's ass about 'they.' All I want is the stupid TUMS."

"Ya seem to have a bit more tension than's healthy. Could give ya them migraines, and there ain't no pain medicine nowhere that'll give you no comfort once them migraines set in. No, siree. It's a horrible pain brought on by tension, pure and simple."

"Look, numskull, all I want is the friggin' TUMS. I don't want your country crap about anything. Just ring it up and let me out of here. I don't want any more talk. Got it?"

"Sure thang. Anythang you say. Now, that'll be sixty-three cent what with the tax and all. We got to pay Uncle Sam his . . . sorry, I ferget you said you don't want to talk no more. Now, let's see. You gave me a five-dollar bill. Zat right?"

"Yes, damn it to hell. I gave you a five-dollar bill. Now move it, molasses mouth."

"Hey, there ain't no use gettin' nasty 'bout it. Now then, that's sixty-three cent, and a penny makes sixty-four, and 'nother penny makes sixty-five, and a dime makes seventy-five, and a quarter makes a dollar."

Antonio clutched his chest. "By heaven, I'm going to die right here in the world's armpit."

". . . Now, that's one dollar, and 'nother dollar makes two, and 'nother . . ."

"Give me the goddamn money!"

Antonio snatched the change from Clyde's hand, stomped out the door, and raced to his car. His stomach was doing flip-flops. Sweat poured down his body. He arrived at his car as the motor coughed and shut down. Steam spewed through the grill and from under the hood.

Clyde leaned over the counter and shouted in the direction of the parking lot. "You just get along back up there to Fi-fi . . . up there to Fel . . . to wherever y'all come from."

A sharp pain rocked Antonio. He clutched his chest and collapsed against his car, sliding down to a sitting position with his back against the front bumper. Antonio pulled in a breath and exhaled for the final time. His heart thumped to a stop as his head slumped forward in death.

Clyde emerged from his store. "Well, now, Yankee, I see you decided to take it easy. Do ya mind if I sit here with you for a spell? My lumbago's been acting up sumpin' fierce. Lucy—that's my wife—Lucy. She's Feral Horton's oldest girl. Lucy says she's gonna fry me up a mess of goose livers and mountain oysters. Ain't nothing better than hog balls for the treatment of lumbago. Say, Yankee, you look a mite peaked. I'll get you a glass of Lucy's nice lemonade. Put a little sumpin' in it for ya, too."

Clyde ambled toward the door to his store. Then, he turned. "Hey, Yankee, don't you go running off nowhere. Ya hear?"

Two minutes later Lucy flounced out of the store. She held a tumbler of lemonade. "Oh, there you are. Clyde said, Doll Britches— that's what he calls me—go fetch that Yankee feller some strong lemonade. Sometimes Clyde calls me Angel Pants. He says my butt was made in heaven. Clyde's so silly. I guess you noticed he talks a lot. I'm kinda shy myself. Sorta like a Cadillac on idle."

When Antonio did not respond, Lucy bent down and touched his neck. She exclaimed, "Why, you're cold as a frog and white as new panties."

Then Lucy screamed, "Oh, my God! Clyde come quick. Clyde!

NO MORE ABOUT JUNIOR

Way down in Brunswick, Georgia on a muggy July morning, Mabel Bohannan parked her twenty-year-old Chrysler on the gravel parking lot at Wilma's Red Skillet Diner. She pushed through the double doors of the country eatery and scanned the dining room for a table. Her nose wrinkled with the pungent smell of grease and collard greens.

Mabel's pretty, round face brightened when she spotted her friend Trixie Wysong in a corner booth. "Trixie, it's good to see you. How ya doing?"

"I'm fine, Mabel. Sit your butt down. I come here a lot. Food's great. Real down-home cookin'." Trixie wiped her chin and tugged on a bra strap. "Yeah, I get breakfast here every Friday. Don't have to fix it for myself and that lazy-ass son of mine. Don't have to clean up, neither. It's the high point of my week."

A gum-chewing waitress of generous proportions approached the table. She sported blond hair with streaks of orange and three-inch mousy brown roots. She yelled over her shoulder, "Tell that bastard I'll get him a refill when I have a second. He'll leave here wearing his coffee if he don't leave me alone." She turned. "What you honey pots gonna be wantin' this morning?"

Trixie looked up. "I'll have Wilma's Sausage Special. And tell Wilma to go heavy on them grits, will ya?"

"You got it."

The waitress pulled a pencil from between her plump breasts. Placing the tip on her tongue, she glanced toward Mabel.

"I'll take the same thing, with heavy grits and all."

"Comin' up."

A short, scrawny guy, grinning like a mule eating briars, brushed past the blonde's ample backside.

"Oh, Big Daddy, it's damn good to see you."

Big Daddy made a blatant, two-handed adjustment and held on until he settled onto a stool at the counter.

The waitress smiled down at Trixie and Mabel. "You girls hear about Big Daddy?"

"Hell, no, and don't you tell us neither. Mabel here's a lady.

She's got refinin'.'"

"Land sakes, you don't say."

"Oh, hell, yeah. She attended Dunbar Middle School and she's been up north and all."

"Do tell. How far up north has she been?"

"Been all the way to Atlanta! Seen the capital and everythang."

The waitress sashayed toward the counter. "Hey, Ol' Big Daddy, Wilma said you'd be back."

Mabel tucked a paper napkin into the top of her blouse. "So, Trixie, I gather that boy of yours is not working anywhere. How old is Junior now, about twenty-two?"

"Twenty-three. And he ain't worth a shit. Dumber than a box of rocks and lazier'n roadkill. The doctors say Junior's perfectly normal. Mentally, I mean. But he still won't do a thang for himself. Always been that way. Thought I'd never get him out of diapers."

Mabel took a sip of coffee. "I recall he wasn't potty trained for several years."

"You *recall* that, do ya? I ain't never ever gonna forget it till my dyin' day. I tried everythang. One time, I didn't change his diaper for a week. He didn't care, didn't bother him one damn bit. I'm tellin' you, Mabel, it was bad, bad, bad. On the third day my old hound dog hightailed it. Ain't never come back. The cat lived for five days in a tree. Five days and she didn't eat a bite. Can't blame her. Who could eat? I tell you that was one pissed-off pussy cat. Stupid cat ain't been right since the day she came down out of that tree. Cat climbs the walls every time Junior breaks wind.

"And my poor old parakeet kept his beak tucked under one wing. Then, on the sixth day, he just keeled over deader'n hell."

"I don't know, Trixie. I bet you could clean up Junior with some strong soap, and he might look right nice. Maybe he needs a country girl to get a hold of him. She'd straighten him out."

"Are you joshin' me? Any decent girl would rather touch a frog. He looks for them girls that don't wash up on any kind of regular basis. Junior hangs around that Shelton girl from down around Piney Woods. Oh, Lardy. If that girl was a whore, she would have to give change back for a dollar."

"Heaven help us, Trixie. She must be a sight to behold."

"Junior's been following his willy since he was a boy. Wherever that thang points, that's the way he goes. One time, when he weren't no bigger than a picket fence, I caught him playing romance with a rotten stump. Talk about a horrible sight. I thought I would faint."

"Oh, my Lord. I bet you about died."

"Yep, thought I would flat-ass die on the spot. But I left him alone. Reckon that stump's 'bout worn out by now."

Mabel shook her head. "At least he's never hurt anybody."

"Hell, no, never will. That boy's scared of the dark. Biggest coward I ever did see."

"Sounds like you have given up on him, Trixie."

"It ain't been easy you know. Tried sendin' him to school. Figured iffen he could learn to read, he could make sumpin' of himself. The teacher said Junior was smart; he just weren't social. Half-assed teacher was no help. She wouldn't listen to nothing about Junior. I tried to teach him his ABC's myself, but he don't know his letters no more than a horse knows when Sunday comes."

The food arrived, and the women dug into breakfast. Mabel blotted a dab of grape jelly off the table. "Junior can't be all bad. I bet he would have a sweet smile if he had more teeth. Walter had a smile to light up a girl's heart."

"Yeah, Walter was a charmer, but Junior is as useless as a gay bull. All he does is eat, sleep, mangle that damn stump, and drink moonshine. Nipples on a boar hog got more worth than Junior. I prayed for that boy every night for years, but it didn't do no good."

Mabel's face lit up. "You ought to send that boy to church. I bet all he needs is religion."

"Tried that. Took him down to Mount Harmony. The preacher said that Junior's done been cursed by the Devil. Claimed Junior wasn't worth churching. Said sumpin' about sins of the father condemning the son. Told me he had never seen a clearer case of Bible prophecy. Said he tried prayin' for my boy, but God don't want to hear no more about Junior."

"Oh, no! Are you saying God has given up on Junior?"

"Preacher swore Junior's got no chance of goin' to Heaven and a slim chance of gettin' into Hell. Preacher don't think the Devil will take him in. I tell you Mabel, I'm gonna lose my mind."

Mabel drained her coffee and motioned for the waitress to refill her cup.

The blonde was chatting away with Big Daddy, all the time brushing him with her hefty bosom and feeling around on his

Tony R. Lindsay

softball-sized butt.

"Say, Trixie, where does Junior get money to buy moonshine?"

"Well, he's got a shit job. Sometimes he mucks out hog lots and horse stalls for farmers. Told you it was a shit job. And he ain't never worked a day without stealing something. He'll steal anything he can carry or drag. And another thang, you can't believe a word comin' out of that boy's mouth. He lies like a rug. He wouldn't tell you his right name iffen he could think of 'nother one. Been that way all his life. And Junior talks nasty about everybody. He would run down the Savior. I tried to learn him right from wrong, but he's as ornery as a hog on ice."

"You kill me, Trixie. I've never seen a hog on ice."

"Well, a slippin' hog is a frustrated beast. He'll bite your damn arm off. I was about to tell you that a bootlegger feller sells Junior the real cheap stuff from the bottom of the cooker—the shit nobody else will drink. Junior can go through a quart of whisky faster than a dose of salts through a widow woman."

Mabel leaned closer. "Let's see if I got this right. You say Junior is bone-lazy, a thief and a coward, a liar, and a heavy drinker with a bad attitude. He doesn't smell good, and the Lord knows he's got some mortifying sexual habits."

"That's about it. When that boy weren't no bigger than a possum, I'd look down at them eyes and know I was nursin' a fool. There was a light on, but there weren't nobody home. Thought I was goin' crazy. It ain't been easy trying to do right by that boy. The damnest thang is, Walter was proud of Junior. Said Junior was a boy after his own heart. Can you beat that?"

"Heavens, no, can't anybody beat that."

"I can tell you more about Junior. Thangs you won't believe."

"No, please don't, Trixie. There's nothing you can tell me about Junior that I wouldn't believe. One thing is for sure, Junior is a special boy."

"He's special, all right. Special stupid, lazy, and girl-crazy just like his daddy. Walter was always chasing women or anything with a pulse. If it breathed, it was fair game for Junior's daddy. Wanda Aslinger told me that she read that men don't stop thinking about sex for twelve minutes after they die."

"Trixie, you can say what you want about Walter, but he was a good-looking man. So tall, so big and strong, and that 'I'm-gonna-

56

nail-ya' grin."

"Yeah, I know. Them charms got him in a lot of trouble. Got him kilt too. I'll say this for Walter, he was a hell of a lover. He could make a girl feel like she'd done been snatched up by a motorcycle gang. I don't know how a man could be in so many places at one time."

Mabel's eyes narrowed as redness spread down her neck. She fanned her face with a wave of her hand. Mabel crossed her legs. Uncrossed them. Then crossed them again. She brushed bits of toast from her blouse.

Mabel's head tilted forward as she skimmed away the last invisible crumb. "Damn, Trixie, maybe we should talk about something else. I'm getting all worked up. My Harold makes a poor imitation of a motorcycle gang. Fact is, he don't measure up to a Boy Scout. But hey, he's good to me, and he works hard every day. I figure working counts for something."

"Damn straight, working counts. Say, Mabel, I got to be heading home. Junior will be looking everywhere for some spending money. When it comes to finding a spare nickel, Junior can pick the fly shit out of the pepper."

ODDWATER

OBITUARY OF JOSEPH C. ODDWATER, JR.
The Ludowici Leader

Joseph C. Oddwater, Jr., passed away unexpectedly Saturday evening. Joe was a deacon, Sunday school teacher, Boy Scout leader and a credit to our community. He was not ordinarily the type of man to frequent strip clubs, but it was senior discount night at Here Kitty Kitty. The program featured lap dances for five dollars for three minutes. Joe's heavy breathing gave way to no breathing. He gasped, grabbed his chest, slid off his chair and died on the floor.

County Coroner, Mortimer Philpot, attributed Joe's death to CBD (Cranial Blood Diversion) followed by acute throbatosis and localized rigor mortis. Undertaker, Paul Moss, expressed concern about the difficulty of closing the body-length lid on Joe's casket.

Left to cherish Joe Oddwater's memory are the management and staff of Here Kitty Kitty. A memorial has been established in his honor. Donations should be sent to Miss Delilah Woodbinder in care of Here Kitty Kitty, 1201 North Broadway.

During next Saturday's performance, customers will stand for a moment of silence, remove their caps and place their right hands over their hearts. Dancers will bow their heads and position their right hands modestly.

Joe will be missed by his dog, Frances, and his wife of forty-one years, Beulah Mae Skaggs Oddwater.

A funeral service will be held at Mount Harmony Baptist Church. Reverend Travis Cody officiating. An overflow crowd is expected. Brother Cody has announced that the coffin will remain open during the service.

Rest in Peace, Joseph C. Oddwater, Jr.

NO TALK

Professional ventriloquist Tobias Yost had barely survived a disappointing gig at the Let Loose Social Club in Atlanta. He packed his slack-jawed dummy Floyd Oakes into an old, black trunk, heaved it onto the back seat, and headed south on Route 23 on a sweltering August day.

A dash-mounted fan with three-inch blades whirled with a monotonous buzz. Window vents poured in plenty of air, but the blistering gusts were scant relief from ninety-eight degrees.

Tobias kept a close eye on the temperature gauge of Bess, his 1936 Ford sedan. Water had to be added to the radiator every fifty miles. Two one-gallon jugs sloshed behind the passenger seat.

The needle pegged against the "H", and Bess screamed for a drink. Tobias pulled to the side of the road in a narrow valley between low hills. He raised the hood to help Bess cool enough to remove the cap from her radiator. Tobias took a red handkerchief and wiped sweat from his bald head. On the slopes above the highway, rail fences ran up and around green pastures in an irregular crisscross pattern. He focused on a lone elm tree about ninety yards away near the crest of a hill. A solitary man sat under the tree with his back propped against the trunk. A dog was stretched out in the tree's shadow. A horse lazily nibbled on short grass while sheep wandered aimlessly. The man, the dog and the horse appeared to be at peace with the world.

Tobias sauntered up the hill. Maybe he could find out how the fellow was able to rest serenely while Tobias scuttled through life like a fiddler crab at low tide.

From a distance of about thirty yards, Tobias could see that the guy under the tree was a shepherd and not the friendly sort. Coal-black hair twisted into braids spilled down his chest. Trails of smoke curled from a homemade pipe. He wore a slouchy, broad-brimmed hat cocked on the back of his head.

Tobias trudged closer, flashing a toothy smile. "Hi, there."

The man said nothing.

"My car overheated, and I need to let it cool down."

No response.

"Care if I sit here with you under this tree for a spell?"

The shepherd continued to whittle on a short stick.

Tobias eased down into a cross-legged position and pushed out a heavy sigh. A minute of silence passed that seemed to last an hour.

Tobias licked his parched lips. "Hot as hell, ain't it?"

Silence.

"I'm Tobias Yost."

Not a word.

"You got a friggin' name, man?"

"Name, Gabby."

"You don't say. What's your real name?"

"Folks call me Gabby."

"But what in hell is your damn name?"

"None of your friggin' business, asshole."

Tobias cleared his throat and extended one leg, keeping the other bent under him. "Would you mind telling me the dog's name?"

"Willard."

"What kind of a dog is he?'

"Good dog."

"No, I mean what breed of dog?"

"All dog."

Tobias chose not to pursue the matter.

"What's the horse's name?"

"Willard."

"What? They're both named Willard?"

"Here, Willard, the *dog*, and over there, Willard, the *horse*. Asshole understand?

Tobias scrutinized the shepherd's features. The guy under that ridiculous hat was probably a lonely herdsman, but he had no interest in talking. Tobias muttered to himself. *Here I am in the middle of God-knows-where, in the middle of a field, talking to an introverted idiot, named Gabby, with a horse and a dog both named Willard.*

An idea sprang into the ventriloquist's head.

"What do you do all day, Gabby?"

The shepherd emitted an exasperated groan. "Get on horse, dog follow, tend to sheep."

"Do you mind if I talk with your dog?"

"Crazy-ass, loco, sumbitch. Dog no talk."

The mutt tilted up his head. Tobias asked, "What do you do all day, Willard?" Then Tobias spoke without moving his lips in a voice between a growl and a bark. "Gabby get on horse, me follow, tend to sheep."

Gabby's eyes widened and his pipe fell from his mouth.

"Mind if I talk with your horse?"

"Horse no talk."

Tobias strolled over to the old mare. "What do you do all day, Willard?"

The horse whinnied, "Gabby get on back, dog follow, tend to sheep."

Gabby's chin dropped to his chest. His eyes stared, unblinking.

"Mind if I talk to your sheep?"

Gabby leapt to his feet. "Sheep lie!"

DECEMBER DAYS

Jebadiah Malinzak was getting old at age eighty-two and proud of it. His daily routine was to sit on a bench in the park across from his condominium and fed popcorn to the pigeons as he watched girls jog past in leotards and flimsy t-shirts.

Jeb had an enduring admiration for girls, but he despised the ubiquitous birds. The noisy, persistent, feathered bandits made an awful mess. The old man had read somewhere that modern birds are descended from fierce dinosaurs. Jeb had long suspected what the ornithologists confirmed.

An attractive young woman jogged over a low hill. She had a bounce to her gait, but precious little movement inside her shirt. Jeb realized the lack of jiggle was due to a bra that could keep Dolly Parton under control on a trampoline.

The girl sped by with her nose in the air and without a glance in the old man's direction. Jeb dropped just enough stale popcorn to entice a fat pigeon to come within range of his right foot, but the bird easily avoided Jeb's attempt at a punt.

Another girl topped the hill. She had the confident persona of a woman who knows she's attractive. A blond ponytail swung left and right. She moved her shoulders in an intriguing manner, pushing her right shoulder forward and bringing it back then twisting from the waist and repeating the same motion with her left shoulder. The globes under her shirt moved up and down as a unit. Jeb was feeling better. He dribbled a whole handful of popcorn onto the ground at the side of his bench as the jogger flashed a brief smile.

She giggled under her breath, "Harmless old men are so cute."

Jeb contemplated the cadence of her shoulders and jiggling bosom. When she passed him, he noted her tight buns and marveled at their movement in perfect rhythm with her swaying ponytail.

"So cute," he muttered.

In the autumn of 2008, Jeb celebrated his eighty-third birthday with a little cake, ice cream, and bourbon. Jeb's children broke the news that he had been dreading to hear. Their application for him to move into the December Days Nursing Home had been accepted.

"You're going to love it, Dad."

"Yeah, r-r-right. Nothing but old folks there and not a damn thing to do."

"That's where you're wrong. They have bingo every day and lots of crafts and stuff."

"Well, if you like it so much, why don't you move in the galdarned place? I'll stay right here by my jogging trail."

"There's no use arguing. You move in Saturday."

With reluctance and foreboding, Jeb left his beloved condo and took a last longing look at the bench where he had evaluated so many examples of feminine athleticism.

December Days was not as bad as Jeb had feared. The food was good, and bingo included a little under-the-table wagering. Women were everywhere. In fact, eighty-one percent of the residents were female, but their conversations invariably got around to the embarrassment of incontinence, followed by details of a litany of surgeries dating back fifty years.

Jeb would have been depressed if it were not for the nursing staff—four "lookers," and several more who were better than passable.

Jeb was proud to be one of the few men in the place who could still tie his own shoes and even touch his toes with a trifling bend of his knees.

Nurse Tricia was especially impressed with Jeb's fitness. She told him how good he looked, why he should stay active, and how clever he was to have the door to his room adorned with only his room number. Most residents couldn't remember their room numbers, so their doors were decorated with pictures of grandchildren, religious symbols, or some other identifying object. Tricia had Jeb convinced he could be the next poster-boy for *Ultra Seniors.*

Jeb spotted his favorite nurse walking ahead of him down a long hall. "Hey, Tricia, how old do you think I am?"

"Why, Mr. Malinzak, I'd say you were about seventy-one."

"Ha. I'm eighty-three years old."

"But, Mr. Malinzak, you're so frisky."

Farther down the hall, long-time resident, Paula Mae Parker, stood at her apartment door—designated by an old, black, go-to-meeting hat.

Jeb sauntered up to her. "Paula Mae, how old do you think I

am?"

"I'm pretty good at guessing age. Don't be surprised if I get it right."

Paula Mae stepped into her room and motioned for Jeb to follow. The old lady sat on a straight-backed chair. "I've got to feel you up a bit if I'm gonna guess your age. It'll only take a minute."

"You've got to be kidding!"

"Nope, I'm serious, Jeb. I've never known it to fail."

"I guess it's okay. I mean if it won't take too long. You know what I mean."

Jeb moved directly in front of Paula Mae. She grabbed his loose trousers and began kneading thoughtfully. "Hmmm. Uh-huh. Yes."

Jeb felt a happy stirring. Paula Mae lifted and twisted Jeb's sensitive parts. "Hmmm, hmmm. It's as I thought."

Finally, Paula Mae released her grip. "I'd say you're eighty-three years old, give or take a few days."

"I can't believe it! That's exactly right. How on earth did you know?"

Paula Mae giggled. "I heard you tell Tricia."

BACK TO BUDAPEST

Hungarian-born Gustav Zweck had been in Philadelphia for three months.

"How's it going?" his friend asked.

"Not so fine. Three months and no snuchie."

"I'm not surprised. Look at you. You got all the muscles of a snail. You're as sissy as a tulip. American girls want he-men. They're crazy about cowboys and bad-boy bikers."

"Never could ride bike. Maybe ride horse."

"Give it a shot, Gus. You might find a cowgirl. Those girls know how to ride. A cowgirl can make a man glad he was ever born."

After another week without affection, Gus suffered two episodes of fainting. Lori Blumenthal was wearing four-inch heels and gathering the spilled contents of her purse from the floor when Gus abruptly lost consciousness.

Then Gus plopped on the ground when Minnie Wilcox said, "Good morning, Gus."

A shaky and desperate Hungarian resolved to learn to ride and booked a five-day stint at Rip Seaman's Ranch about an hour's drive outside of Dry Gulch, Wyoming.

***

"Howdy, partner. What's your name?"

"Call me Gus."

"Yo, Gus. My name's Rip, and this here's Six Pack. A mighty fine hunk of horseflesh he is."

"Vay too big. Don't vant to go far."

"Yeah, Six Pack is a big boy. It's rough country and twenty miles is all you need. Just remember to yell 'Go' if you want to go faster and 'Whoa' if you want to go slower. You got it, Gus?"

"Ya, ya, got it."

Rip gave Six Pack a slap on the rump. "Off with you, tenderfoot."

Six Pack lunged forward and Gus looked as if he might throw up. "Voh!"

Now 'Voh' sounds a lot like 'Go,' and Six Pack began to canter.

"Voh, seggfej, voh!" (Whoa, asshole, whoa.)

69

Tony R. Lindsay

Six Pack bolted into a gallop.

"Szenazabalo artany " (Hay-burning bastard.)

"Ya voh, ya voh, ya voh, ragasztot egy bankot." (Something about a gluepot.)

Six Pack sprinted into top gear.

"Hivatkozas megkerdojelezhoto tenesztesi." (An impolite reference to questionable breeding.)

Gus dropped the reins and held onto the saddle horn with both hands.

"Do-do agy." (Do-do brain.) "Baratsagtalan szo anya." (Unkind words about Six Pack's mother.)

The horse raced across terrain that would challenge a goat.

"Ya voh, nagyanja volt a lo nem ereny." (Six Pack's grandmother was also a horse without virtue.)

Six Pack splashed through a shallow creek and charged up a steep slope.

"Rossz kozerzet a keves mozgart tartalmazo es akkor enokeini soprano es paradezik mint egy kanca." (Bitter complaints about his own testicular discomfort and plans for a slow-motion surgical procedure that would have the stallion whinnying in soprano and strutting like a mare.)

Gus hung on until Six Pack finally turned for the barn and pulled up in front of a bale of hay.

The shattered Hungarian with battered balls had both feet on the ground at last.

"How did it go, partner?"

"Megy vissza Budapest. Boven snuchie, lehet kapni nelkkul lovaglas sarkany segget agesz pokol." (Going back to Budapest. Plenty snuchie and you don't have to ride a damn dragon's ass all over hell to get it.)

IVORY BLUE

Things were looking up for Al Duszynski, and it was about time. Selling kitchen gadgets and humane mousetraps house-to-house for twelve years barely earned him enough money to support his habits. But all that was changing. Al had discovered Ivory Blue Laundry Detergent three weeks ago, and he was pulling in big bucks, smoking thick cigars, and drinking Chivas Regal.

Selling direct to homeowners can be a tough way to make a living, but the fringe benefits are unbeatable. Ringing doorbells in the middle of the day gave Al plenty of opportunity to comfort lonely widows and provide solace to women with traveling husbands.

Al hadn't come across a lonely widow in almost a week, and he was feeling constricted. However, the prospect of tapping a swanky new neighborhood kept him going.

"Good morning, Ma'am. I hope you're having a great day. My name is Al, and I'm here to show you something really wonderful."

Al tried to gauge the reaction of a plump, pretty lady in her early forties. But he did not detect any signal that she was interested in him or his product. He knew his best strategy was to flash his pearly whites and say nothing more until she responded.

"I'm sure whatever you have is the best of its kind in the world."

Touché. Maybe she didn't mean to respond with an innuendo. Al was not sure.

"Young lady, I have the most amazing new product to come along in twenty years. I'm privileged to represent a laundry detergent that will soon be famous all over America. Allow me to present the incomparable Ivory Blue."

"I'm sure it's fantastic, but I don't have a lot of time."

"A quick demonstration standing right here on your front porch will require almost no time, and you will be astounded."

"What is it you want?"

"I have a plastic bowl here and a bottle of water. Would you bring me the dirtiest item in your home, for example—a dust cloth? I will prove that Ivory Blue works with incredible speed."

"Well I do have an old sock that I use to clean behind the refrigerator. Do you think Ivory Blue can handle that?"

Tony R. Lindsay

"I'm sure of it."

The lady brought a rag covered with dirt and lint. "Okay, let's see what you can do."

"It's no problem, I assure you. Just watch this."

Al poured water into the container and added a small amount of Ivory Blue. He held the cloth by two corners and plunged it into the bowl while chanting a well-rehearsed jingle:

Dippy, Dippy, Do
In Ivory Blue
Test With Your Nose
Smells Like A Rose.

Al sniffed the sparkling white cloth and held it in front of her nose. He waited for her reaction.

"That's amazing! Why, it looks and smells brand new."

Al had taken a big step toward making a sale. "Do you have anything dirtier? You will be surprised at what this stuff can do."

"How about my garden gloves? I use them all the time, and they've not been washed in years."

"Bring 'em on. Ivory Blue will clean the dirt out of those gloves."

The lady produced a pair of soiled gloves embedded with grass stains.

Dippy, Dippy, Do
In Ivory Blue
Test With Your Nose
Smells Like A Rose.

Like magic, the gloves were as clean and fresh as the day they were purchased.

"Oh, my goodness, I can hardly believe my eyes. I've never seen anything like it."

Al bubbled over with excitement. One more demonstration and it would be time to ask for an order. "I'm almost finished. Do you have something really, really filthy?

The lady blushed and looked around furtively. "I have one item. But you must promise that you won't tell a soul if I show you what I'm talking about."

"Great. I love a challenge. I won't breathe a word to anyone."

"This is kind of embarrassing. We went on a camping trip way back in August, and I wore a single pair of panties every day for

72

eight days. I discovered them yesterday in the bottom of the clothes hamper."

"Hot dog! This should be good."

She scurried away and returned with a pair of panties that were originally white. Now, they were a kaleidoscope of colors. A pale blue mold thrived near the waistband. A dark green fungus encircled the leg-holes.

Al used the tips of his fingers and thumbs to grasp the panties at the seams. The murky, 2-ply crotch dangled stiffly.

Al turned his head to the side. He tried not to breathe. "Okay, here we go."

Dippy, Dippy, Do
In Ivory Blue
Test With Your Nose . . ."

"Uh . . . . "

Dippy, Dippy, Do
In Ivory....

NEVER GONNA MAKE IT

I'm Reverend Jimmy Joe Swigit, and I'll share with you a gospel-truth story about the early days of my ministry before I gained control over the lust that racked my body and ruined my testimony.

Pastor E. Allen Wilcox had announced his retirement. Mount Harmony needed a new preacher, and I needed a job. So, on the first Sunday in April, I was guest minister at the venerable Baptist church in Ludowici, Georgia.

I stood on the pulpit talking with the saintly old minister before the beginning of services. His soft southern drawl was like maple syrup oozing over hot biscuits.

"Preach-ah Swigit, Ah' make a welcomin' address, and then call on yawl to deliver Gawd's message to the good people of Mount Hah-mo-nee. Yawl can sit heah by our esteemed Deacon Seaman and converse in the spirit of the Lawd."

I took my place on a throne chair and looked out over rows of empty benches. Deacon Seaman nudged my elbow. "Reverend Swigit, I want to tell you something about our church. We're very liberal, and we welcome everyone to worship with us."

"Praise God, Deacon Seaman. I'm a liberal man myself."

"Yes, I've heard some stories. You should know that a special lady attends services with us every Sunday morning, and I don't want you to be surprised by her appearance. She dresses inappropriately and is known to place a price on her affections. But Lotta Mae Daniels is a sweet person.

A few seconds later, I poked Deacon Seaman. "Hope you don't mind my asking, but does she charge varying prices for varying affections?"

"Reverend Swigit, I'm sure you jest."

It had seemed like a reasonable question to me, but I let it pass. Then I spotted a lovely, dark-haired woman entering the church. I prodded Deacon Seaman. "Is that Lotta Mae?"

"No, that's Mrs. Roberts. She teaches one of our Sunday School classes."

I looked her over. "Kinda nice, don't you think?"

Deacon Seaman ignored my comment.

Worshipers began filing in. I noticed a lissome beauty wearing a low cut blouse and flashing a beaming smile. Flowing red hair covered one eye and spilled over her shoulders.

"Deacon, is that Lotta Mae?"

"No, certainly not."

I watched as she laughed and chatted with some church ladies. I couldn't help myself. "Deacon, do you suppose she's a *real* redhead?"

The deacon's jaw dropped. He glared at me. "Reverend Swigit, that's my wife!"

"Oh, sorry. Beg your pardon." A few seconds later, I leaned closer to the deacon. "So?"

"So what, Preacher?"

"So, is she a real redhead or not?"

I figured he would know, but he appeared to be choking.

Then it happened. A blond temptress waltzed down the aisle, dressed in a white micro-skirt and a thin blue blouse with cleavage from here to Halloween. She wore five-inch spiked heels and displayed legs that reached from the ground to heaven. Her hips flared in a perfect heart-shape. As she came closer, I heard sultry music in my head. "Ka-boom, ka-boom, ka-boom."

I got a little excited. You know, like special excited as she sashayed down to the front pew and sat right in front of me. She crossed her legs as if she was wearing blue jeans on a camping trip. Well, I got really excited. A cat couldn't scratch my enthusiasm.

I shifted my position and turned sideways to the congregation before focusing again on Lotta Mae. From somewhere in the foggy distance I heard, "We're gonna ask Rev-on Swigit . . ."

I tilted my head a little more to the right. There! Something seemed to peep back at me.

Then, it was that darn voice again. "Rev-on Swigit, please come faward and lead us in a word of prayer."

My ardor reached unprecedented heights.

"At this time, Rev-on Swigit."

Huh? Say what? Oh no! God no! You can't do that. I mean I can't do that.

Pastor Wilcox peered over his shoulder and spoke through clenched teeth. "Get up heah now, Swigit."

I closed my eyes and asked God for a miracle. God said my wish could be granted, but my relaxation would be permanent.

Holy cow!

I told God, "Forget it. I'd rather be humiliated than maimed."

The anxiety of the moment put me in a somewhat improved condition. I glanced over at Lotta Mae as she made a positional adjustment on the hard pew. Instantly, I regretted my decision to look in her direction.

The pastor's face reddened as he glared at me. Murmuring among the audience began to swell. I signaled for the pastor to approach me and lean over so I could speak into his ear. "Pastor, I can't stand up."

"Why not, brother?"

"Well, I'm already standing like a tin soldier, if you know what I mean."

"Oh, Ah see."

"That's what I was afraid of."

"Boy, I'm gonna give you a pass on that prayer, but I'll tell you sumpin' right now, son."

"Yes, sir?"

"Yawl never gonna make it as a preach-ah."

KITTY GREEN

I'm Reverend Jimmy Joe Swigit. It's good to be here again tonight among God's people. I see Brother Al and Sister Wendy in our midst. Glad you could be with us. God be praised. This evening I will tell you about the occasion of my second visit as Guest Minister at Mount Harmony Baptist Church.

I sat on a throne chair beside Deacon Seaman prior to the opening prayer.

"Deacon Seaman, does that lady who bestows her affections on sinners and saints for a price still attend services every Sunday?"

"No, she has moved on to the nation's capital, but one of her colleagues, Miss Kitty Green, is even more devout."

"What can you tell me about her?"

"Well, Kitty is a gorgeous woman and more than a little sexually active."

"Yeah, that's the kind I like."

"Really Reverend Swigit, you should avoid earthy comments. Now, I must tell you there is something special about Kitty Green."

"What's that?"

"Kitty gives twenty-five per cent of her earnings to our church. You understand I don't condone her lifestyle, but she spreads a lot of good cheer among our congregation.

A minute or two passed until a sweet young thing pranced down the aisle and sat down, tucking her dress in behind her knees.

"Is that Kitty Green?"

"Certainly not. That's Connie Kullberg. She's an usher."

"You don't say. A gusher is she?"

"Are you deaf? I said, 'Usher.' She helps people find their seats."

"Yeah, sometimes I could use a little help myself."

Then a really fine woman made an appearance.

"Is that Kitty Green?"

"That's Jennifer Volt. She's speaking to the Seniors Group this afternoon, and she will make another speech tonight. Jennifer is an orator."

"She's a what?"

Tony R. Lindsay

"She's an orator."

"Yeah, that's the kind I like."

"Reverend Swigit, I find your sense of humor disquieting."

"Hey, she's disquieting me, I can tell you that."

"Preacher, you are incurable."

"What about that woman over there?"

"Oh, that's Linda Williams. She's a missionary."

"Really. That's a little vanilla for my taste."

Deacon Seamen threw up his hands and shook his head.

"Tell me more about Kitty's financial contributions to the church."

"Well, first of all, her services are expensive. She charges fifty dollars—per minute."

"Saints preserve us! I could drop a hundred bucks—maybe 150."

"I told you she's expensive. Walter Lewis had to get a second mortgage. The old fool said it was worth it."

Deacon Seaman acknowledged a few parishioners as they took their seats.

"Our church would have a budget shortfall every month if it were not for the generous nature of Kitty Green. Last month she provided more money for our Community Outreach Program than Bingo or Ms. Hall's bake sale."

"My word!"

"In December, Kitty insisted that every client on her list make a $500 donation to the church to preserve their anonymity. We were able to pay off the new addition to our sanctuary."

"That's wonderful, Deacon. The Lord works in mysterious ways."

"Yes, but I'm sorry to say that Kitty's earnings and contributions have fallen off drastically in recent weeks."

"Oh, no. What's the problem?"

"Well, there's a rumor Kitty is spreading more than good cheer in our community. We've had an epidemic of social disease and church attendance is down twenty percent. Also, Kitty feels real bad about what happened to one of my fellow deacons, Gerald Lowe."

"What happened?"

"It's like this. Poor Gerald passed on a vicious infection to his wife. I can tell you that Gerald Lowe was one of our finest deacons, God rest his soul."

I was thinking about the unfortunate Deacon Lowe as I gazed at a large stained glass window. Sunlight cast a rainbow of colors over the pews. Then I caught the scent of expensive French perfume. My mind flashed back to my Navy days--*I'm lounging among the bikinis in Old San Juan.*

I looked around to see a captivating beauty wearing a short skirt and six-inch heels. She made Serena Williams look like a boy.

Blood rushed from my head. I felt faint.

She took a seat on the front row with her shapely legs arranged in a most immodest manner.

"Is that Kitty Green?"

Deacon Seaman leaned toward me and took a closer look. "I can't be sure, but I think it's the way the light's shining on it."

ORCHESTRA MUSIC

Welcome to the third monthly meeting of the Greater Ludowici Men for Media Decency. I'm Reverend Jimmy Joe Swigit. We thank the Lord for this big crowd tonight.

Margie and I used to love to go to the movies. Films were about action and romance. We were intrigued when the hero and his lovely co-star came to a moment of intimacy. Violin music flooded our ears and the camera panned up to the sky. A crescendo of orchestra music culminated with a clash of cymbols. The audience took a collective breath and let out a long, drawn-out "AHHH."

My sweet Margie and I went to so many movies when we were courting that we expected to hear violins on our honeymoon. But, hey, that's enough about me. We're here tonight to bring decency back to the theater, television and the printed word. Somebody say "Amen."

"Amen, Brother Swigit."

Movies used to be romantic, uplifting and almost spiritual. Today, we must bear witness to every thrust. In days gone by, the heroine would coo in a soft voice, "Do you love me?" Now she asks, "Do you have protection? There are some blue ones on the desk. I got a few green ones, and a couple of those funny-type ones."

The starlet used to look longingly into her lover's eyes. "I want the moment to last forever." Nowadays she says, "Hope you don't mind if we step on it. I've got a manicure in twelve minutes and it's a block away."

I remember when the camera zoomed in for a close-up of Grace Kelly's delicate ear as she dabbed on expensive perfume. Today, if the camera were close to her ear, her foot would obstruct the view. I tell you it's disgusting. I'm appalled every time I watch it.

We're here tonight to abolish filth. Every man who wants to put an end to explicit movies and television and get back to the days of orchestra music, please stand up.

I said, "Stand up."

I said, "Get on your feet."

Come on, guys, somebody stand up.

VIAGRA FOR THE SOUL

Some folks don't have to wonder about God. They have all the answers. Television preacher Vinny Hindquarters is a charming man with a heart of platinum. Vinny is inspired, no doubt about it. He says God's children are supposed to prosper, and Vinny prospers greatly. His manner is not pretentious, but he does wear suits that would be the pride of a Mafia don. Vinny gives credit for his worldly success to God. I like a humble man.

I never miss a broadcast of Pat Rump and the 900 Club. What I would really like to see is Pat Rump on the Vinny Hindquarters Show. Wouldn't that be a hoot? Maybe Pat could be a guest speaker. It would be fun to see Vinny and Pat get into an argument over some point of scripture. Something like, "Are we all going to have the same reward in heaven, or will there be better accommodations for really good people?" I'm thinking that Mother Teresa should get a better recompense than my Uncle Jack Doggins, a life-long tyrant. I was told that Jack made a deathbed profession of faith just minutes before sailing into heaven. Reverend Hindquarters could explain to lesser folks like me the ultimate fairness of the matter.

No one has a clearer understanding of the mind of God than the immensely popular John Haghebe. He's the fat fellow on television with billboard-sized signs to illustrate his sermons.

My favorite sermon was Viagra for the Soul. Haghebe's display for that one featured the Washington Monument in the background, along with a picture of the famous Wachovia Building in Winston-Salem, North Carolina, and a moon rocket taking off from a launch pad. The missile appeared to be advancing at a 45-degree angle. I thought rockets were launched straight up, but Reverend Haghebe knows exactly what he's doing. He designs those signs himself with guidance from an even higher authority.

Reverend Haghebe told his graying and balding audience that he was sure most of them were aware of the miraculous power of Viagra, a blessing from God for aging Christian men. The miracle drug is also a benefit for Christian women, indirectly, according to the preacher. He went on to say that the truth shall make you free. Truth is connected in some way with Viagra. I didn't understand it, but I'm sure Pat Rump and Vinny Hindquarters would know exactly what their colleague was talking about.

Preacher Haghebe said God values nothing more than truth. It is incumbent on all of us to tell the truth no matter how much it hurts. That practice has brought him closer to God on a number of occasions, such as when he called the hulking Governor of California a filthy womanizer.

During a recent sermon, Haghebe invited anyone in his congregation who had not been truthful with God to come forward and make things right before it was too late. A skinny fellow who had seen better days ran down the aisle and fell at the preacher's feet. The poor man was on the verge of a complete breakdown.

"Brother Haghebe, I have sinned."

The portly preacher helped the man to his feet. "Sir, if you will tell God and the anointed children of God gathered in this temple about the sins in your heart, you will be forgiven."

The distraught soul groveled and bawled. Between sobs he said, "Preacher, I'm a drinker. I drink a beer every day, sometimes more. Please forgive me."

"It is God who will forgive you, sir. I am but a humble servant. Pour out your heart and direct your pleas to God."

The chap produced a red handkerchief and blew his nose with considerable zeal before stuffing it back into his pocket and resuming his confession. "Well, God, you ain't gonna like this."

"Look heavenward, my son."

"Yeah, right. God, Thou knows that I lust in my heart something awful. I mean like all the time. Thou must know what I mean."

Haghebe turned to the audience. "God loves an honest confession."

"Well, God, I might as well tell you the worst part."

The tormented soul bubbled and choked. Tears streamed down his face. Hundreds of parishioners reached for tissues.

"God, you know what I'm gonna tell you. You know I slept with my wife's sister."

The audience gave a collective gasp. John Haghebe clutched his chest. The desperate sinner dropped to his knees. "God, it was great, the best ever. Please forgive me."

Reverend Haghebe snorted, "God will forgive you, son, but your wife is going to kill you."

***

All this thinking about God has caused me to wonder. The Man Upstairs could be a woman. We've all heard about Mother Nature, and it's logical that the one who gave birth to all life should be female. God might be a white woman; lots of folks are white. God may be an Asian mother; women from the Orient are so pretty. However, in the absence of a direct divine revelation, I've concluded that God is a large black woman, nurturing and stern.

"Boy, you get in this house. I'm not going to tell you again."

Once inside, strong arms engulf you in a warm hug. "Soup's on, baby."

FULL CIRCLE

In the beginning, Mother God created the heavens and the earth. Eons drifted by and She was content to take long naps and sing in an off-key soprano. Then Mother God designed a simple form of life and observed as one-cell creatures evolved into complex flora and fauna.

Mother God would have loved to chat, but there were no women around. So, Mother God created Eve. They lived together in a lovely garden and babbled daily for millennia. But Eve became bored and unhappy.

An apple tree grew in that garden. Mother God took a branch from the tree and fashioned a toy for Eve in the image of a one-eyed snake. Eve was ecstatic.

Eventually, Eve became bored again. Mother God looked with pity upon Eve and gave a form of life to the snake, attached Adam to it, and presented Her gift to Eve.

Eve's euphoric dancing flattened a portion of the garden.

The blissful existence of Eve and Adam lasted for a while. One day Eve complained to Mother God that Adam was so large and powerful that he threatened to dominate her.

"Don't worry, Eve. Men are stronger than women, but women are smarter. I planned it that way. It's something I call parity."

Time passed and generations of humans began to slowly multiply and evolve.

At first, men hunted by charging a wooly mammoth or a giant bear while flailing away with clubs and rocks. Many men were torn apart or trampled. Then men learned to hunt by setting traps and using strategy to bring down their prey. The planning and execution of their hunting schemes resulted in men developing improved cerebral function. With brains almost as large as women, and with much stronger bodies, men exerted dominance over women for thousands of years. Females had to resort to sly and indirect methods of getting men to behave in an acceptable manner.

Generations rolled by and men began to depend upon flint-tipped spears and to rely less on out-thinking their quarry. The brains of men reverted to the time when they were far less intelligent than women. A significant portion of the male brain migrated down his torso, lodging in a lower appendage.

And so it came to pass that women reclaimed their original position as the superior gender. Mother God looked down upon creation and was pleased to see that Her plan had come full circle.

Almighty Mother God announced in a wind blown all over the world, "As it was in the beginning, is now, and ever shall be, women rule the earth."

GONE BUT NOT FORGOTTEN

Discount Day for seniors at Ludowici Beer and Wine, and I stood on the sidewalk fumbling for my frayed AARP card. Then my eye caught something riveting about the tailgate of a new black Cadillac Escalade.

I moseyed over for a closer inspection. A dozen portraits stared back at me. Snapshots of guys from about fifty-years-old to eighty-five plastered the rear window. Some of the faces were smiling and friendly. A few appeared to be terrified. Most displayed the narrowed eyes and crooked grins of lecherous old fools. Below each face was the caption, *"Gone but not forgotten."*

I was examining the pictures when a beguiling beauty in her mid-forties approached the gleaming SUV. Her pale, flawless skin required no makeup. Dark hair cascaded over her shoulders. In spite of making no apparent effort, she was an eyeful. Gorgeous gave me a polite smile that was all the encouragement I needed.

"Pardon me, ma'am. The photos on the back of your vehicle fascinate me. Would you tell me what they are about?"

Her lovely face flushed as she lowered her head. "Yes, I will tell you, sir. Those are pictures of friends and acquaintances that have elevated to a spiritual realm."

The time was not right to ask why only men were in the montage. "And you put their photographs on your Cadillac?"

"Yes, it's my way of remembering them."

She took a black lace handkerchief from her bosom and dabbed cat-like, icy blue eyes.

My heart melted. My ardor grew. She was not wearing a bra. "It's a fine idea. You are obviously a special lady."

"I don't think I'm special, but some people say I'm unique."

"How so?"

"Some people say I'm a witch. So many people around me have died unexpectedly."

"That's ridiculous."

"Just the same, that's what they say, and it distresses me."

I was convinced she was not wearing panties. My mind flashed back to two women I have known who never wore underwear. They were warm-hearted, affectionate, generous and enthusiastic girls. I was determined to prolong the conversation. "Dear, you shouldn't listen to that type of person. The undereducated class believes in vampires, witches, sorcery and all that nonsense."

She dabbed her eyes again. "I agree with you, but some of my most intelligent friends make awful comments."

I sucked in my gut and popped in a mint. "What you need is a more refined, intellectual companion."

"Thank you. You seem like such a sensitive man."

"And you, darling are a beautiful woman."

"I'm afraid I must leave now, sir."

She pulled out her keys.

There was no time for additional forays. I had to make my move, say something clever and urbane. "Maybe I could buy you a drink. I mean, if you drink. You know, alcohol. Uh, it's not like I wouldn't buy you a Pepsi or something."

"No, I must go. But I'll always remember your kind words of encouragement."

Another wildly attractive woman would walk out of my life forever.

She unlocked the driver's side door. The vision in black turned to me. "Thanks, again."

Then she hesitated.

This could work out yet. I pushed my glasses up on my nose. Then I licked the palm of my hand and gave my comb-over a wet swipe.

She reached into her car and pulled something from a black box. An enchanting smile spread across her face. "Do you mind if I snap your picture?"

OL' POSSIBLE

The truth is, sixty-something years ago, I was a precocious and exceptionally good-looking boy. My mother said her only child was the cutest kid she had ever laid eyes on. And smart, too. Her baby had blond curls, big brown eyes, and the most radiant smile in the neighborhood. No family had a child as lovely and clever as Momma's little darling.

One of Momma's favorite stories involved me running up to her babbling about the activity of my little kitten. "Hurry, Momma, come see what Hugo's got."

"I'm busy. Can't you just tell me?"

"Hugo's got your fat holder."

Momma followed me to the back porch to find my kitten tussling with her lacy new bra.

"See? I told you."

During my pre-school years, I continued to be brighter than any of my playmates. Jokes that passed over the heads of my friends were not lost on me. Mrs. Webb, our aging neighbor, told Momma that she almost fell while taking a bath. Momma urged the feeble senior to be careful and inquired as to how she went about taking a bath.

"I wash up as far as possible, and then I wash down as far as possible. Then, I wash possible."

Momma and Mrs. Webb guffawed. I sniggered, too. Mrs. Webb said, "Don't worry, Ethel. That boy is too young to understand what we're laughing about."

I spouted, "It's good to know that, after all these years, Ol' Possible still gets a soaping now and again."

"Tony."

"Yes, Momma?"

"Shut up."

My first-grade teacher failed to notice my advanced mental abilities. In fact, she told anyone who would listen that I would never progress beyond elementary school. Arithmetic was my best subject. I was a whiz at adding single-digit numbers, but adding double-digit numbers befuddled me. When I could no longer add with the aid of my fingers, I resorted to guessing at the answers. The teacher was no help. She said something like, "When adding numbers above ten, you have to record your nominal number and transport your dual digit to the left."

"Say what?"

Spelling was my real downfall. I tried to remember that when spelling "cat," the "t" follows the "a" which is preceded by "c." I got a lot of low marks and could have become discouraged, but Momma would engulf me in a warm hug. "Don't worry, son. You're almost a genius and cute as a Beagle puppy."

School was a drag, but I enjoyed wide-ranging discussions with Momma. She mentioned the effects of wind blowing across bent grass and holding kites aloft. Momma gazed into the distance. "I wonder where the wind comes from and where it goes."

I stared at her earnestly. "Momma, even I don't know that."

Momma passed away many years ago, and I still miss her. When I struggle to balance the checkbook or consult with *Spell Check* after every paragraph, I know Momma would understand.

A person can get through life with a rudimentary aptitude for math and abysmal spelling skills. It's not easy, but it's possible.

PRETTY DARN CLEVER

Going on eight-years-old, my curiosity about girls was killing me. Otis Lee Harper was six months younger than me. I could talk to him about girls or anything else. One summer day, we took a break from tossing a football around in a field behind my house.

"Otis Lee, bet you don't know what I heard."

"Whadja hear?"

"Can't tell you."

"Aw, come on. Spit it out."

I moved closer. "Yesterday, I was playing marbles over at Larry's house."

"Yeah, go on."

"His big brother, Jerry, was playing basketball with a bunch of kids near our marble ring. They were talking nasty."

"Momma told me to never talk nasty. Hurry, what'd they say?"

"They were talking about that Dinwitty girl and how pretty she is, and how they would like to kiss her and stuff like that."

"That's dumb. I would never kiss a girl. What else did they say?"

"You ain't gonna believe it, but Wally McClain said he would like to wear Debbie Dinwitty's underwear."

"What? He let the other guys hear him say something that stupid?"

"Yeah, I almost fell over when Wally said he'd like to get into Debbie's panties."

"Craziest thing I ever heard."

"Otis Lee, I've got it pretty much figured out about where babies come from."

"We already talked about it. They come from their mother's belly."

"Yeah, but I mean how they get out."

"Tony, if you know, you've got to tell me."

"They come out from, you know, down-there. But I'm not sure if it's from the front down-there or the back down-there."

"Listen, Tony, promise me you won't ask me how I know what I'm gonna tell you."

"Cross-my-heart-and-hope-to-die, I won't ask you how you

know."

"They come out from the back down-there 'cause there's almost nothing up front."

"How do you know?"

"I told you not to ask me."

"Okay, I'm sure you're right. We're pretty smart to figure out where babies come from."

"Yeah, we're smarter than most boys, and smarter than any girl."

"You got that right, Otis Lee. But we still don't know how babies start growing in the first place. You want to hear my idea?"

"Okay, lay it on me."

"There's always a baby in a girl's tummy, but it doesn't start growing until a guy sticks her down-there, and that starts the baby getting bigger and bigger."

"Oh, my Lord!"

"I'm pretty sure that's it. That's what the big boys were talking about."

Otis Lee looked down at the ground and shook his head. "No, that ain't right."

"How can you be sure?"

"Daddy might do something like that, but Momma wouldn't do nothing like that in a million years."

"My Momma wouldn't do that, either. But when she was younger, before I ever knew her, maybe she would do stuff. The big boys say it takes nine months once a baby starts growing until it pops out. Getting married has something to do with it. I figure when a guy and a girl get married, it takes about a year for them to get over the shame and work up to doing something nasty. Then, nine months later, bingo, the baby pokes his head out and takes a look around."

From fifty yards away, we heard the pounding of a basketball onto a dirt court and shouts of the fellows choosing sides.

Otis Lee grinned. "Say, let's go see if Larry wants to play marbles."

I got my bag of marbles, about forty, and met Otis Lee at Larry's house. Larry was eager to play "keepers." When a marble was knocked out of the ring, the shooter got to keep the marble and shoot again. Larry had almost a thousand marbles. I knew we would leave Larry's with fewer marbles than when we arrived, but a few marbles would be worth it to hear the big boys talking about girls.

Sure enough, the guys were discussing Debbie Dinwitty and a girl named Ellen. They all agreed that Debbie had the cutest butt in Rule High School and maybe the best fanny in the world.

The big boy's called Ellen "High Handles."

Frank Miller, a skinny kid with lots of yucky bumps, said Ellen was a tallywacker teaser. In my mind, I could see Ellen with a feather teasing Frank's thing. Guess it wasn't much fun. Frank didn't like Ellen one little bit.

I watched my marbles tumble one by one into Larry's big box.

Over on the basketball court, the big boys spat every few seconds. They made lots of adjustments. A bunch of guys used the "S" word. Some fellows even said the "F" word right out loud. If my Mom had ever heard me say that word, my punishment would have resulted in a trip to the hospital.

Otis Lee was wiped out and my last nine marbles tumbled out of the ring with what Larry described as a pretty good run. He told us to come back when we had more marbles.

We headed for my house.

"Otis Lee, do you think Frank really had his junior tickled with a feather by that girl they call High Handles?"

"Are you kidding? No way. She would not give that guy air if he was in a jug."

"Yeah, you're right. Big boys are dumb. It's not easy to figure out girls and babies and that stuff. We're pretty darn clever. You know that?"

GOD BLESS MISS FINCH

My first venture into the realm of hormonally influenced judgment occurred in the fifth grade. My class went on a field trip to a local fire station. I made sure to be directly in line behind Miss Finch, my lithe young teacher. When she climbed a spiral staircase, I was following her. She wore a sunshine-yellow pleated skirt. A thin petticoat of stiff, white, lacy material caused it to balloon outward. I turned my head heavenward to peek under her dress.

Holy moly!

Exposed to my gaze was the sight most avidly desired by boys, yet the most denied. Her nylon stockings reached above her knees, held up by straps that became lost in clothing near her waist. Above the stocking tops I saw the inside of a woman's thigh. She wore white, nearly transparent, panties. Secreted within those flimsy, silk threads reposed the nameless "*it*."

Jeepers, Batman and Robin!

When she realized I had stolen a look under her dress, her face reflected surprise, then amusement and finally a smile that twinkled into to a mock scolding expression.

God bless Miss Finch, wherever she may be.

ATTITUDE

I dated only girls who were nines or tens. The secret to my system was that I awarded three points for attitude. A six with a great attitude was a nine in my book.

Then I discovered that women have their own rating system. I met a girl in a bar and after four drinks she confided that I was an eight. I felt pretty good about that. Then she explained her system. I got one point for being a male and one point for walking upright. I got two points for not carrying a concealed weapon. Her system awarded one point for a man with an English accent (I missed that one) and one point for a man with money (I missed that one, too). But I got one point for making her laugh and three points for a mustache.

She asked if I would buy her another drink.

"Are you sure you need another drink?"

"I need a drink. I'm trying to drink hair on your head. And I'm trying to drink your belly flat."

"Okay, but tell me now if you're going home with me or not, damn it."

She laughed. "In your dreams, bucko."

I said, "In my dreams you would have to take a number. You would not be in the top one hundred."

Well, it didn't work out. I went to my apartment, crawled into bed, and snuggled with my Teddy bear.

Two nights later I had my sights set on a nine. I took her to dinner. I think she could sense my financial condition. She ordered a Value Meal. I didn't want her to think that I was completely broke, so I told them to Supersize it. I told her that I was not hungry, but I got an extra straw and shared her Pepsi.

After dinner we walked eight blocks to her apartment. Would this be the night when I would end the longest drought of my life? I think she could sense my desperation. We stood in front of her apartment door. She looked up into my eyes. "I've had a wonderful evening filled with sexual tension and excitement. But it was not tonight."

NOBODY EVER TELLS ME ANYTHING

You will not believe what a friend told me today. After all these years, somebody finally explained it. I didn't know. I just learned that when a woman says *Drop Dead*, it means she really likes you.

I didn't know that! Nobody told me.

When I was single, girls stood in line to tell me to drop dead. Now I realize that those women were crazy about me. When I think about all the cuddling I missed, I want to cry.

If I had known how women really felt about me, I could have been as popular as the singer Tom Jones. There I was living in a bone-dry desert of affection, and he would strut onto a stage wearing white pants that were spray-painted on his nether region. He would croon, and the girls would scream and spasm. Then he would ooze into a rocking motion of his hips. Delirious females would throw their panties at his feet.

And me—sleeping with a Teddy bear.

Did you ever wonder how those girls kept their jeans on and got their panties off?

The floor was littered with lace and itsy-bitsy thongs. If those girls had thrown their silks to me, I would have snatched them in midair and taken those ditties home. And I would still have them. The only treasures in my humidor are old cigars.

A friend of mine is seventy-nine-years-old and has more girlfriends than Carter has pills. "Wilbur, how do you do it? Why do women drape all over you?"

"It's because of my incredible sexual stamina. I can go for two hours."

"You must swallow a boatload of those little blue pills."

"Nope. I wear a jockstrap soaked in starch. When that jockey comes off, I'm as ready as a bull elk."

Twenty minutes later, I picked up a jock strap and a three-pound box of starch at Costco. The girl at the checkout counter asked, "What are you going to do with all that starch?"

"I'm gonna soak my new jockstrap in it."

Tony R. Lindsay

"Oh dear, it will be as stiff as a poker."

See what I mean? Everybody knows about starch but me. Nobody ever tells me anything.

WHERE TO LOOK

"This is your first night in Philadelphia, and it will be an evening you will never forget." Alan winked at Kathy and continued, "We're going to take you for a Philly tradition. Are you ready to get started?"

"Can't wait," I said in my slow Southern drawl.

We strolled one block before pushing through the doors of The Pale Raven. Alan and Kathy were greeted by a dozen of their drinking buddies. Alan announced in a loud voice that they had in tow a good ol' boy. Someone pushed a cold pint of ale in front of me. I was soon telling them about life in the South. Then I learned it was time for the whole crowd to move on to another pub. We strode into The Swan and Her Sisters. A fat guy put a pint in my fist. I said, "Back home, we don't drink ale. This stuff tastes like it came straight from the horse. Good ol' boys drink moonshine, and we do a lot of coon hunting where I come from. We get 'bout ten hounds and sit around a campfire and listen to the dogs howl as they tear through the woods. A coon hunt ends when someone says, 'Gather around boys. It's time to pee on the fire and call in the dogs'."

Someone shouted, "Sounds like fun."

Meanwhile, Alan matched me pint for pint. I knew he was drunk because I could see two of him. I spied a girl standing in the back of the crowd. She had purple spiked hair with red tips. She wore a "hauler" top and low-rider jeans. And tight. If she had a nickel in her pocket, you could see if it was heads or tails. She wore a dog collar and a leash that hung to her knee pads. She had rings in the tops of her ears. Her eyebrows and nose were pierced. I called to her. "How you doin', honeypot?"

She gave me a Philly salute. I said, "I love your piercings. Whatcha got? Five piercings?"

She yelled, "Eight."

I made a quick count. Then I said, "No. That ain't right. I'm quite sure there're five."

"And I'm quite sure there are eight."

I noticed that among the tattoos on her belly were two arrows pointing inward and downward. I yelled, "What's the matter with you Philadelphia fellers? You guys need directions? We know where to look. If you guys need directions, you probably need instructions, too."

Kathy put one of my arms around her shoulders. Alan put my other arm around his shoulders. Kathy said, "We got to get you out of here."

They half dragged me to their crib. I mumbled, "Take me to the bathroom." I stood there at the toilet with my arms around their shoulders. Finally, I said, "Kathy, Alan, I sure appreciate this."

Then I muttered, "Take me to the extra bed."

Kathy said, "We don't have an extra bed."

I began to panic until Kathy guided me to the sofa. She put a pillow under my head and covered me with a blanket. She told me "Nighty Night."

NEVER RAMBLE

My motto is to never ramble and always hammer home the essence of any story.

Essence is such a lovely word. The final "e" sort of slips off the tongue leaving an aftertaste of something sensual. I recite the word slowly with my eyes closed....

A raven-haired beauty peers seductively from behind a velvet screen. Her sly smile hints, "Come hither, beeg boy." A fat Mexican guy sits under a huge sombrero, a chin string hanging loosely about his neck. He flashes a wicked smile that reveals a gleaming gold tooth. Polished bullets attached to leather straps crisscross his chest. Farther down, a pearl-handled pistol and sinister curved dagger are shoved under his belt. In the background, shadowy, unsavory men lounge on overturned barrels and lean against dark doorways.

Don't walk. Don't run. Get on your horse and ride, baby, ride!

What's this about a horse?

If I had a steed, it would be a black, shiny stallion about the size of one of those Clydesdales that pull the beer wagon at Christmastime. Have you noticed that horses have really small ankles? A horse's ankle is not much bigger than a man's ankle. I mean here is a creature weighing more than a ton, standing on ankles barely bigger than mine. You are probably thinking a horse has four ankles, twice as many as Homo sapiens.

You're right, of course, but I still think horses have piddling ankles.

Did I mention Homo sapiens?

What's a sapien anyway? And how do we know they were homosexual? Beats me. But I bet you've already thought about gay sapiens, like when you were ahead of me regarding a horse having four legs and, consequently, four ankles.

I didn't mean to be redundant about the ankles thing. It just kind of flowed out while we were considering the romantic inclinations of sapiens.

Now that I've got you back on track, you're probably wondering why modern man is not descended from the Hetero sapiens, or maybe the Bi sapiens, or even the Tri sapiens. Those Tri sapiens will try anything. But—Homo sapiens? How can it be? Your question makes sense to me, although, at this point, my concurrence may provide you with little comfort.

"No comfort at all," you say.

Perhaps you're a little unsettled realizing that we are thinking along the same lines. If you've been rambling about beguiling senoritas, horse's ankles and the sexual proclivities of our earliest ancestors, you are right to feel uneasy. You need help.

GRANDMA,
SPEAK TO ME

My grandmother would have died on the spot if she had been watching television with the family and was suddenly confronted with an amazing new cure for an intimate itch or a splendid new stool softener. Most people long for the days when the world was a more innocent place. We watched *Gunsmoke* without fear of advertisements popping up for a personal lubricant that warms to the touch.

I can see Grandma now, knitting by the fireplace with the grandchildren scurrying around her feet. A teenage granddaughter and her boyfriend play Monopoly. The whole family is watching *The Lawrence Welk Show*. Mr. Welk announces that he will be right back after a word from their sponsors.

"This message is brought to you by Flo-Mo for Women, the exciting new cure for your balky bladder. Do you remember, ladies, when a trip to the bathroom was like tipping over a bucket? Does your tinkle sound like a man's? Flo-Mo is the answer, but Flo-Mo is not for women who are nursing, pregnant or fooling around.

"If you are overweight or underweight, you should not apply Flo-Mo more than once per day. Side effects include nervous indigestion, night sweats, nosebleed, diarrhea, cold sores, nausea, swelling, blurred vision, joint pain, spotting, body bruising, sleeplessness, vomiting and foot odor. Women should pay close attention to changes in their sexuality. Secondary effects range from a complete loss of libido to god-awful perversions such as equestrimania. Until you know how Flo-Mo affects you, avoid cheap champagne and Barry Manilow albums.

"You should not apply Flo-Mo if you cannot sit or stand for three hours. Minor effects include bloating, genital warts, bone loss, premature aging, and liver spots. Social consequences include confusion, depression, and regression, such as an overwhelming urge to throw food at your sister. Notify your doctor if you experience spontaneous and thunderous flatulence accompanied by feelings of anxiety and loneliness. Let your doctor know if you are no longer welcome to sing in the choir.

"Serious side effects include tremors, hemorrhoidal proliferation, and hallucinations. Deaths attributed to Flo-Mo are often instant and painless. Lingering deaths are rare and should be reported.

"Try Flo-Mo and be sure to consult your physician if you develop an unsightly rash, have difficulty swallowing, loss of appetite, or anal atrophy."

Grandma just died!

Actually, Grandma fainted and is revived in time to see a medley featuring some underpaid musicians.

"Ah, wunnerful. Ah, wunnerful. We'll be right back."

In the next commercial, two ladies talk in hushed tones over cups of coffee. A third woman waves a greeting. The two ladies immediately stop talking and welcome their friend with fake smiles. A man appears from behind a large potted plant and looks directly into the camera.

"Are your friends talking about you behind your back? Can you be sure? Try our new feminine fragrance, Lily Lady. Think of the confidence you'll have when you smell like a flower."

Grandma begins to swoon again. The grandchildren rush to her aid with a glass of water. She lapses into unconsciousness and misses a commercial featuring Dr. Blazemore and a miraculous new cure for hair loss. The commercial features a bald dude, friendless, depressed and merely going through the motions of life. Then he tries Dr. Blazemore's Grow-Mo for Men.

Shazam!

He has hair and more female company than any one man ought to be allocated. Fetching, scantily-clad beauties fall all over him. He starts to earn a lot of money. Life becomes exhilarating.

Fiddlesticks. I know for a fact that hair loss for men is caused by an overabundance of testosterone. That's the stuff that makes a man a man. Excess testosterone causes hair to disappear from a man's scalp. However, the hormone creates manifestations of maleness that would be the envy of those poor slobs with hair. Growing hair is a waste of good hormones. Guys with hair on their heads are the same fellows who need Erect-Mo.

I'm sure you've seen those commercials featuring Erect-Mo. A middle-aged chap directs us to tell our physician if we experience arousal for more than four hours. Four hours! Four hours is a long time—even for a bald guy. For some of my friends, four hours is a career. If I ever have an erection lasting four hours, you can bet I'm going to tell my physician—and everybody else.

Meanwhile, Grandma is fully recovered from her fainting spell and resumes watching television. She is revived in time to see a commercial for Sleep-Mo for Women.

A lovely lady touts the benefits of a good night's sleep, but she warns us that all sleep medications carry some risk of dependence. She flashes a broad smile and adds that instantaneous, debilitating addiction happens with no more than one in four first-time users.

"If you develop sagging limbs or collapsed lungs, these could be signs of a serious medical condition. Tell your doctor if you see anything green."

What was that?

Grandma, speak to me!

SWEET REASON

I leaned back in my recliner with a beer, chips and a bologna sandwich. I'm devoted to an activity that floods my mind with knowledge and wisdom.

My first selection was "Sex and The City." A hormonally-charged, middle-aged woman complained about the youthfulness of her new love interest. "Hardly old enough to shave, but old enough."

Interesting stuff. But there had to be something more educational.

A click of the remote produced the answer to my quest for enlightenment. The star of "Reverend John Haghebe Today" impressed me as a man with all the answers. In case you've missed John Haghebe, he's a rotund fellow who speaks with great authority.

Something annoys me about television evangelists. Why must they s-h-a-r-e their experiences with us? Why don't they just tell us what happened? I wrote down the address to send a donation for what the clergyman referred to as "sowing seeds." Haghebe assured me I would reap a bountiful harvest from the garden of his ministry. Checkbook in hand, I began to write when the preacher announced his intention to *share* one more story. That was it! I tore the check in half and reached for the remote.

My next stop was Black Entertainment Television. Where do they find so many gorgeous and friendly women? Each female was brimming over with affection and better looking than the last. The problem with BET is they feature more ugly dudes than alluring ladies. There's another thing. I can't understand a word they're singing. Without the guys and without the music, BET would be a wonderful channel.

I moved on to "The 900 Club." Pat Rump is my kind of guy. He knew before any of us that Hurricane Katrina was an example of the wrath of God. I applaud a man with the courage to match his convictions. But, to be honest, I wish his pronouncements were a little more aligned with sweet reason.

The remote slipped from my lap and fell to the floor. I retrieved the gadget and tried to select another channel, but the darn thing refused to move away from Pat Rump. Could it be divine intervention?

I finally managed to click through several more channels until I came to "Blue's Clues" on the Preschool Network. The show features a sissy boy and his cartoon dog. I try to be modest but, frankly, I didn't find the program intellectually challenging. After about twenty-five minutes, I clicked some more.

My attention peaked when I landed on a channel featuring "Body Shaping by Bonnie Sue." She's always in a good mood as she encourages her audience to keep up an impossible aerobic pace. Bonnie Sue smiled and bounced and jiggled in the most unassuming manner.

After a careful review of 104 channels, I settled on The History Channel, The Travel Channel, Arts and Entertainment, and any program on The National Geographic Channel.

But what I really want to see is Bonnie Sue in white tights.

THE NOBLE SNAKE

My wife swears that any snake, no matter the size or stripe, is a shoulderless fiend lurking in ambush. Snakes without venom kill by the cruelest method of all—*sheer terror.*

She lays into me. "What men like you don't understand is that most fatal heart attacks occurring outdoors are caused by the slimy, slithering sadists."

"But, dear, snakes aren't slimy."

"They are, too! The only good snake is one that has been dead for a month, and I wouldn't touch it with a stick."

"Honey, why don't snakes have a right to exist?"

"Why don't birds fly backwards? Because they don't. That's why."

"But, baby, I'm not sure you're being reasonable."

"My brother has more sense that you. He says that snakes can hear him coming, and the sight of one causes his butt to want to chew grass."

"Yeah, he's a clever guy. No doubt about it. By the way, snakes don't have ears. They don't actually *hear.*"

"R-r-right. And frogs don't actually *jump.*"

A wise man would get out of this conversation, but I push on. "All snakes are not evil. We owe everything, even the procreation of humans, to a venturesome snake."

"How can you say such a thing?"

"Hear me out, dear. In the beginning, Adam and Eve ran around in a lush garden called Eden. The lovely Eve was bare-butt naked, but Adam paid her no attention. A humble snake lived in Eden—a garden snake. The poor snake didn't have a pit to hiss in.

But he was big on sin. After an apple-tasting episode, Adam began to notice Eve. A wiggle here and a jiggle there awoke a localized stirring of Adam's anatomy. Ever since, we've had sin and sex, and we owe it all to that noble serpent. Snakes are just another one of God's creatures."

Her eyes narrow; she purses her lips. "That's just what they want you to think."

"Who?"

Tony R. Lindsay

"Snakes, for heaven's sake."

"Oh, silly me."

Her voice moves up an octave. "Snakes are not the creation of God or nature."

"But, sweetie, are you sure about that?"

"Absolutely."

"I'm afraid I don't understand."

"And I'm not surprised."

Her eyes squint to mere slits. "The slithering demons fled from the nether regions of the underworld to stalk helpless women and *dull, mindless men.* Snakes were spawned by Satan."

Pushing my luck, I ask, "Where would we be without that original snake? Without sex we would not have had all the generations that have followed Adam and Eve. I risk a little pinch. "And you and I would not have those tender moments that we enjoy."

"That's it! You don't understand a darn thing about snakes and not much about anything else. I'm not speaking to you. And you know what I mean."

CHINESE MATH

"Hey, pal. Good to see you. I hear you've been taking those once-daily pills that have you ready when the moment is right."

"Yeah, but what they don't tell you is that you'll be ready when the moment ain't right. Take last Sunday. We were sitting in church and they were passing the offering plate down the row. A dime fell from the plate and landed on my lap."

"Oh, no."

"Yep. Bingo."

"What did you do?"

"The lady on my left tried to hand me a songbook, but my wife beat her to it."

"What happened next?"

"We waited until the service was over and everyone had left the sanctuary. Then I put the songbook away and picked up a folding chair to carry with me to the car. Wouldn't you know it? We ran into the preacher in the parking lot. He said, 'Brother Lindsay, what are you doing with that chair? You look like a lion tamer.' I said, 'You could say that.'"

"Man, that must have been embarrassing. I bet you never go back to that church."

"Yeah, we're going back. They want me to sing in the choir."

"You in a choir robe—in your condition—that's something I've got to see."

"Things got worse on Wednesday. My team won the Ultra Senior Men's Softball Championship. I was in the showers with a dozen other guys. Then I thought about the time when I was in high school and we were on a bumpy hay ride. Julie Koontz rode on my lap. Thought I was in heaven."

"Hut-o. You shouldn't have thought about that. What happened?"

"What do you think happened? Two seconds and Junior was as hard as Chinese math. I toweled off and got dressed. But before I left the building, the coach slipped me his number."

"Guess you're not going back to that team."

"No, I ain't going back."

"Holy cow. Anything else?"

"Yeah. Just this morning my wife was standing on her tiptoes to reach a box of cereal."

"Don't tell me. B-I-N-G-O."

"That's right. I could drive a nail with it. The next thing I heard was a voice saying, 'Sir, I'm going to ask you to leave.' It was the manager at Kroger's."

"I'm glad I talked with you. I'm not ever going to take one of those pills."

"I don't know. Sometimes I think it's worth it."

NO DERBY FOR ME

The sumbitch stabbed me with a butcher knife in my own bed. I raised my arms to ward off the next thrust, but he was content to twist the blade inside my abdomen. Screaming, I tried to find my attacker in the dark. But I couldn't locate a hand or arm, or handle protruding from my belly. I reached for the light switch beside my bed. I was prepared to stare into the face of a deranged killer, but the light illuminated not a soul. I searched for a gaping wound. I couldn't believe my eyes—nothing. Yet, horrible pain emanated from deep inside my body. Something was dreadfully wrong.

Moaning with every wave of agony, I picked up my bedside phone and punched in the number of my neighbor. "Phil, this is Jake. I'm dying!"

"What?"

"I'm dying, I tell you. I think my stomach ruptured or my backbone snapped."

"I'm on my way."

Phil rushed to my apartment. "Jake, what the hell is the matter with you?"

"There's no time to call an ambulance. You got to get me to an emergency room."

Phil drove my car as I lay on the back seat doing my best to make peace with God. Would a man be held accountable if he was born with a low resistance to temptation?

Phil skidded to a stop under the canopy of St. Luke's Hospital. Two burly guys heaved me onto a gurney. Nurses secured my arms and legs and rushed me down a long hallway. I faded in and out of consciousness. Fluorescent lights passed overhead. Then, strong lights became even stronger. Heaven was going to be brighter than I had imagined.

A man with a round face tried to rouse me. "We're going to give you something for the pain and to help you sleep."

Sometime later, an angelic fellow in a gleaming white garment gazed at me with compassion. I figured it was Saint Peter but the nametag read, "Dr. Juan Momera."

"Feeling better?" he asked.

119

My head cleared. I was still on the earth side of the Great Divide.
"We're going to take care of you. You have a kidney stone."

"A kidney stone? You mean I'm not dying?"

"Well, I'll be surprised if you die tonight."

"Oh, thank God."

My relief was short-lived. Dr. Momera announced his perverse intentions. "We're going to perform a basket extraction."

"You're going to do what? I thought for a second you said *basket* extraction."

"That's what I said. We'll insert a tube, with a basket on the end of it, up your urethra all the way to your bladder. Then we'll extract the stone b-a-a-a-ck down the tunnel."

"Wait a minute, Doctor. There's been some mistake. You have me confused with some other guy. Any extraction that involves a basket ain't gonna work."

"You'll be fine."

"Doc, you got to listen to me. I didn't run in any derby last year. Nobody threw a blanket of roses across my back. You understand?"

The slow-witted, sadistic doctor said nothing.

"Doc, listen, damn it, to what I'm telling you. See these feet? They are size eleven, not much bigger than average. Know what I mean? I'm telling you any extraction with a friggin' basket, for Heaven's sake, ain't gonna work."

"Relax. Wait right here."

"Where the hell am I going to go?"

He returned with a sturdy, bubbly forty-something nurse. "I'm Elizabeth Lantz."

"So?" I said.

Another physician and two more nurses entered the room. The whole damn gang was interested in my case.

Ms. Lantz looked down at me. "We understand you are somewhat apprehensive about the basket extraction of your kidney stone."

"You could say I'm somewhat apprehensive. You could say I'm fuckin' terrified! I tried to tell this pillar of urology that he has me confused with a more fortunate fellow. What you have here is a veterinarian reject from Churchill Downs. Read my lips. It ain't gonna work."

"We have some experience in these matters."

"Don't you understand that I could be maimed? My life with Little Man could be finished. If you use that stupid basket on an ordinary bloke like me, I may require transplant surgery within a month."

"Please try to relax. You won't feel a thing."

"That's what I am afraid of!"

"We'll have you under general anesthesia."

"Well, that's a comfort. I figured you intended to give me a bale of hay to munch on."

The witless doctor said they were going to increase the medication in my drip line and put me to sleep. I appealed to Ms. Lantz. "Look at my hands. These are not the hands of a power forward in the NBA. Understand?"

The jolly nurse was going to be of no help.

Dr. Momera nodded to the anesthesiologist. I tried to protest, but... Zzzzzz....

I woke to see the fine figure of a lady, clothed in white, on her tiptoes reaching up to pull something from a high shelf. This time I was in heaven for sure.

She turned to face me. "It's all over."

"Do you mean the operation—or the use of my precious willy?"

"Willy-willy, no problem. You'll see."

"Yeah, I'll see, but it won't be anytime soon."

"Prized willy-willy okay. No worry."

"I prefer a single willy, if you don't mind."

I attempted to shift my position. "Did you get the blasted stone? Did you get the bugger with a basket?"

"Si, Senor. You want to see?"

"Sure."

She presented a teensy, wicked-looking pebble about the size of four grains of sand clumped together. Razor sharp edges protruded in all directions.

That afternoon, Phil and his voluptuous girlfriend, Charlotte, came to visit me.

"How you feeling, sweet baby?" asked Charlotte in her molasses drawl.

"I'm okay, but my lower region is numb."

Phil howled. "What else is new?"

Charlotte gave him a disapproving stare, but Phil continued to enjoy his pathetic little joke.

I told them how brave I'd been under the circumstances.

Phil smirked. "How big was the stone?"

"About the size of a marble, smaller than a ping-pong ball."

"Yeah, a lot smaller. Let's see the stone. You've gotta have it."

"Sure, but they have it down in the lab. They're going to put it in their trophy case."

Charlotte placed one hand over her heart and the other on my arm. "Oh my, sugar pants, I just love big, strong men with courage."

I whinnied and nuzzled her hand.

SLEEPING WITH A LIGHTNING BUG

Decades of close observation, intense contemplation, a few brain lapses, and one resounding success have qualified me to dispense my knowledge of women to less experienced men.

The first mistake young men make is to assume women aren't much different from guys. Women are just female people, right? Wrong. Dead wrong. It's more complicated than that. Dr. Joyce Brothers said there are many differences in men and women other than the most obvious and cherished ones. She got that right. Women are different.

For example, many women don't love football. Let's say you're watching your favorite team on television. It's fourth and goal; the championship is on the line; two seconds are left on the clock. The commentator is about to lose his mind. Your wife walks into the room with the phone in her hand. "Mother wants to talk to you."

"Now? Tell me you don't mean now."

"Yes, Mother wants to talk to you now."

"Dear, you know I worship your mother, but ask if I can call her back."

"I knew it. You don't like my mother. She was right about you."

You turn your attention back to the television as the announcer shouts, "It's all over! What a play. In thirty years of broadcasting, I've never seen anything like it."

A man tries not to cry.

The only real maven I have ever known on the subject of women is my old buddy, Wally Whitfield. In my high school, all the guys said if you want to know anything about girls, ask Wally Whitfield. I had not seen Wally in twenty years when I ran into him in a pub downtown.

I bought my amigo a beer and reminded him of the time when we were in the tenth grade and had a brilliant idea for a prank to play on an unsuspecting woman. A historical farm near our neighborhood attracted many tourists. The homestead included an old-fashioned outhouse that had continued to serve its original purpose. Wally and I

Tony R. Lindsay

hid a tape player behind the privy and set it to be activated by the opening and closing of the toilet door. The recorder was left blank for a few seconds to give the women time to settle onto the seat. Then Wally's voice screamed, "Hey, lady, we're working down here!"

As luck would have it, the first woman to enter the potty was Wilma Dean Holbrook, the preacher's wife. We waited behind a woodshed and listened as she locked the sliding bolt. Exactly nine seconds later, the door to the loo almost came off the hinges. She leapt out and scrambled along a path toward the parking lot. She tried desperately to get her silks in place, keep her dress down, and run like hell—all at the same time. Her face was the incarnation of the famous painting, "Scream."

Wally remembered the incident in every detail. He bounced around the bar mimicking the woman's face and her tussle with her underwear. I whooped and cackled, along with the bartender and about a dozen boozehounds.

When the tavern had settled back down, I learned that Wally had mellowed, but was still philosophical about women. "I've been married twice, and I've had trouble with both marriages. My first wife left me, and the second one didn't."

Wally took a swig from his glass. "I've discovered that the best way to cure a nymphomaniac is to marry her. The first thing that you have to understand is that the nature of women can't be explained in words."

"Thanks, Wally,that clears that up. By the way, didn't you marry Kelly Wilshire right after we graduated from high school?"

"That's right."

"I would like to ask you a question."

"Shoot."

"When y'all got married, was Kelly a virgin?"

"Yeah, sure. Absolutely. I mean, more or less. Come to think of it, she did seem to know exactly what she wanted."

I waited as Wally ordered another round and resumed his dissertation. "When it comes to women—I'm talking about the real gems—God only makes about a hundred per year, and they're spread all over the world. Face it. You got almost no chance of finding one and, if you did, she wouldn't give you as much as a smile. God used to make a lot of perfect women, but it doesn't happen much

124

anymore."

Wally drained his glass. "Sometimes I think there ought to be something better a man could marry."

"What have you got in mind?"

"Something with the body of a porn star. Yeah, and enthusiasm. Something with the enthusiasm of, well, a porn star. And the personality of a Labrador retriever. Take my dog, Goldie. She wags her tail every time I come into the room. She's a kissing fool, and Goldie doesn't care if I pet the neighbor's Rottweiler."

"Sounds good to me."

Wally took a deep draft from a fresh beer. "Some guys prefer solo sex. A fellow doesn't have to take a bath or brush his teeth, and there's no woman to yell at you if you fall asleep right away."

"You're right, Wally. Solo has some advantages. But it could be embarrassing if a guy is discovered snoring after a session, and he hasn't properly stowed away. It happened to a guy in Valdosta when his wife and five of her girlfriends decided to move their all-night card game to his house at around midnight. The six women strolled into the family room where an adult film was flashing on the television. Empty beer bottles littered the floor. He awoke to hear his wife yelling obscenities and her friends howling with laughter. The next day, the whole town knew what had happened."

"Damn, Tony, that's an awful story. I hope it never happens to me. It reminds me of Uncle Earl Whitfield who was so bashful he couldn't even talk to girls. Then he ran into a problem with his solitary sex life. He enjoyed eating Cheese Puffs while studying the "Lingerie and Foundation Apparel" section of the Sears, Roebuck catalog. Uncle Earl said he didn't know why at the time, but his member gradually turned orange. It glowed in the dark--like sleeping with a giant lightning bug."

"Your uncle had a problem. The truth is I've never been good with girls. When I was single, I tried everything. I would meet a girl and tell her in great detail about my previous conquests. But nothing happened. I had to try something else. One night I went into six bars and tried to pick the lowest hanging fruit. I told every woman I met that I was a virgin and had only two hours to live. Can you believe it didn't work? Every damn one of them wished me good luck. Sometimes I think women don't trust men."

Wally exhaled deeply. "Yeah, it's a shame."

"There was the time I went to the beach to meet girls. You guessed it. I put a banana in my trunks. What a disaster! Girls would not come within thirty yards of me. After an hour, I figured out that the banana was supposed to go in the front."

"I bet the traffic picked up when you got that banana in the right spot."

"Well, I did do a little better. Wally, I recall that when we were in high school, you had more luck with girls than all the other guys put together. What's your secret?"

Tony, I've never told anybody my secret. But I'm going to tell you."

Wally looked around. He leaned closer. "Mostly, I just beg."

"That's it? That's your secret?"

"Yep, I beg."

"Damn, Wally. I've been doing it right all along."

SLOWLY—AND IN ONES PLEASE

Have you noticed how bold female bank tellers have become? Yesterday, I went into the bank and walked up to the counter. There, staring back at me was a baby's butt in a push-them-up bra.

"Hi-ee, I'm Dana," she said.

"Hi-ee, I'm Cody Walker."

"You're not Mr. Walker. You're Mr. Lindsay. You're teasing me."

"I'm teasing *you*!"

She asked, "What can I do for you?"

I lied. "Nothing comes to mind."

"This is a bank. There must be something I can do for you."

"Well, you can start by cashing this check."

"How do you want your money, Mr. Lindsay?"

"Slowly—and in ones please."

She punched some numbers in her computer and opened the cash drawer while I clung to the counter like Garfield on a window. I'm sure she didn't realize she was bothering me. Women are so gullible.

The girl in the booth next to us knew what was going on. I know that she knew because she giggled. Women have better peripheral vision than Magic Johnson.

The darn push-them-up bra must have been uncomfortable. She tugged at each bra strap in turn. I thought I was going to faint.

I took my money and started for the exit.

"Bye-ee, Mr. Lindsay."

"Tootle-Do, Dana."

I told a friend of mine about my experience at the bank. I told him I was thinking about putting my comb-over in place and asking her out.

He said, "I don't like your chances. Besides, a man your age and a young girl like that—it could be dangerous."

I sucked in my gut. "Hey, if she dies, she dies."

WE OWE IT ALL TO UGG

Not everyone knows about Ugg, but he was the most important human in history. Ugg's tribe, isolated for centuries from the major branches of hominid evolution, lived near a river eons ago in what is now southern Georgia.

Ugg made his home in a cool, dark cave. Sunlight penetrated the entrance for about fifteen feet from sunrise until early afternoon. The den was the only home Ugg had known since his father was banished from the tribe and his mother died of a mysterious illness.

Then one day his father perished attempting to evict a bear from the cave.

The giant beast had been mortally wounded by a spear and soon breathed his last.

Ugg removed the bear's tough hide with a sharp stone, washed blood from the underside, and made a loincloth for summer and a heavy robe for winter. Ugg ate raw bear meat, softening the carcass by pounding it with rocks and soaking it in water.

After a few days, the taste and smell of rotting bear meat had become insufferable. Ugg armed himself with an axe, a spear and a flint knife, and set off on a hunting trip with the knowledge that a hunter could quickly become the hunted; carnivores of every stripe kept the human population few and scattered. Two days away from his cave, Ugg had eaten nothing more than a small fish, a hare, three frogs and a handful of wild berries. Lightning danced in the sky. He gazed up into angry clouds and whiffed the scent of smoke. Soon fire closed in around him. Ugg's throat burned and his eyes watered. He took refuge by wading several yards into the middle of a wide, shallow stream.

Ugg saw a panicked antelope become wedged between a boulder and a tree within a few feet of the safety of the water. Tongues of flame lapped at the creature's legs. It struggled valiantly, only to slide deeper into the crevice. Smoke and fire engulfed the doomed animal.

The wind subsided and a light rain began to fall, extinguishing much of the blaze. Ugg waded out of the stream and approached the charred beast. He ripped a chunk of meat from the animal's hindquarters. With the desperation of a starving man, Ugg stuffed tender, tasty venison into his mouth.

Ugg cut away a fist-sized hunk from the shoulder. The front portion was not burned as badly as the rear quarter, and the flesh was difficult to chew. Ashes continued to flicker near Ugg's feet. He tossed the tough meat into the fire, then found a stick and punctured a smoking, dirty chunk holding it above the flames. Ugg alternated between blowing on the meat and waving it over his head. He could wait no longer for his meal to cool. Ugg placed bite-sized nuggets in his mouth from the tip of his knife.

Delicious.

Ugg trekked back to his cave lugging the rump and forelimbs of the roasted antelope. He also toted a skin-bag of smoldering embers. Back at his sanctuary, he piled dry branches and built his very own bright, warm fire. Although early humans in other parts of the world had been using fire for centuries, Ugg was the first of his branch of humanity to control fire.

Ugg was eating well, but life provided little satisfaction. He was lonely. As time went on, Ugg wandered farther from the safety of the cave, spending several days and nights foraging and hunting. One morning, several miles from his lair, Ugg heard human sounds coming from over a low mound. He sprinted to the top of the hill and hid in thick brush. He observed a woman and a ripe, comely girl digging tubers from the soft earth. Ugg scanned the area as far as he could see in every direction. No men protected the women.

The girl lagged behind the older woman by about thirty yards. Ugg crept to a position behind his quarry and dashed out of the undergrowth. He snatched her with his right arm, holding his left hand firmly over her mouth. She was only half his size, and he easily lifted and carried her back over the hill. She kicked and scratched, but he made sure she did not scream.

Ugg ran with his treasure for a quarter of a mile before he put her down. She was determined to yell. Ugg brandished his knife and eased the tip of the blade into her abdomen, piercing the skin. She gazed down as blood began to ooze. The girl made no more noise. Ugg pushed her in the direction of his cave. A slight jab in her lower back set her to walking at a brisk pace.

Three hours and several miles later, the girl made it clear that she would rather die than go another step with her captor. She would not budge.

Ugg used a strong vine to secure her hands behind her back. Ugg tied a strip of bearskin over her eyes. Another strip muffled her protestations. He hacked a six-foot shaft from a tree and lashed her to it; using vines laced into cords, and began dragging the pole with the girl firmly attached. Two hours later Ugg was exhausted, but the girl still refused to travel on foot.

As the bottom end of the rod slid over fallen limbs, Ugg noticed that the rolling logs made progress much easier. He placed short lengths of wood under the pole at every opportunity.

In the late afternoon, Ugg stopped to rest. He cut two short, round segments from a log and, using his axe, hacked holes in the center of each disk. By inserting a length of wood through the holes, Ugg fashioned an axle. He kept the disks in place by tying vines around the shaft, and then he tied the spindle to the pole that secured the girl. When the journey resumed, Ugg was the first of his branch of humanity to make use of the wheel.

Two bone-weary travelers finally arrived at Ugg's cave. When he released the girl's bindings, she could hardly move. Ugg left her lying on the ground and rushed into his cave. Before leaving on his venture two days earlier, Ugg had built a long line of slow-burning oak twigs on a bed of damp leaves. Three feet of smoldering ashes still glowed with heat. Ugg constructed a roaring fire and charred several chunks of meat on the tips of short sticks. He filled two wooden pots with water from the river, and began to nurse his prisoner back to health. That night he slept between the girl and the mouth of the cave to prevent her escape. But he did not force himself upon her.

She continued to regard Ugg as a pitiless viper, but the cave was comfortable and the meat the best she had ever tasted. Besides, she was aware that Ugg tried to please her at every opportunity.

The couple settled into a routine. Ugg spent several hours each evening carving a menagerie of forest animals, each about the size of one of his thumbs. He would not allow the girl, whom he had named Uggee, to watch the progress of his craftsmanship. She pretended not the slightest interest in his project.

Two weeks into their life together, Ugg held aloft a necklace of twenty small creatures. He gently draped the charm around Uggee's neck. She looked up at him with a tenderness he had not seen before.

One day, Ugg scrutinized Uggee as she picked apples from a tree near the cave. She stood on her tiptoes to reach the bright, red fruit. Ugg noticed that her legs and buttocks tightened each time she stretched high for an apple. The time had come to increase the intensity of their relationship.

But first, Ugg had an idea. He fashioned wooden shoes with his axe and knife. The soles were about four inches thick at the heel and sloped downward to the toe. Strips of hide served as straps. That day marked Ugg's third great invention.

He indicated that Ugee should replace her fur moccasins with the new footwear. She playfully put them on her feet. Uggee took tiny steps prancing around unsteadily. The effect on Ugg was immediate. He looked at her with a mixture of genuine affection and raw lust.

That night began a relationship that would last twelve years and produce nine children. Ugg lived to the age of thirty-eight. Slowed by the rigors of a hard life, he was killed by a bear, perhaps a descendent of the bear that had killed his father.

Ugee and the children buried Ugg far back in the bowels of his beloved cave. There, his bones remain to this day. The greatest man of all time, buried in an unmarked grave.

The three most significant inventions in human history are the control of fire, the wheel, and high heels. And we owe it all to Ugg.

GETTING OLDER

"What hill? Where? I don't remember any hill," my friend said.

"It's called the proverbial hill. And you're over it."

"Hey, I'm still tarp as a shack. Once I was really good. Now, I'm really good once."

"Once in a blue moon," I howled.

Getting older is a lot of fun for guys. We enjoy telling a buddy just how pitiful he appears and how his physical condition has deteriorated along with his mental abilities. Then we brag about our own vigorous life. My amigo, Jack DuVall, is sixty-eight and a few months younger than me.

"I don't know, Jack. Sometimes I look at you, and I wonder if I've passed my prime."

"Ha! You passed your prime when Lyndon Johnson was President of the United States."

The older we get, the more we enjoy pointing out the other guy's deficiencies, and especially the old boy's waning sexual powers.

Women are different. They don't put their girlfriends down, at least not to their faces. If older women talked to one another the way men do, it would go something like this:

"Marilyn, is that you?"

"Yes, Marge, it's me. How have you been?"

"I'm doing fine. This morning I baked cookies for the grandchildren."

"That's right. You *are* a grandmother. Looks like you have put on a few pounds. Maybe it's those cookies that you've been baking. The ones for the grandchildren."

"Actually, my weight hasn't changed much."

"Yeah, r-right. But now that you're getting older, you need to cut back. You look frumpy to me. I'm sure you are heavier than last year. Turn around."

"Honestly, Marilyn, I weigh the same as I did in high school. Of course, I was always a big girl. Maybe I have augmented some curves, but I've still got it. You know what I mean?"

"I know exactly what you mean."

"You go, girl!"

"Our husbands are lucky."

"They sure are, but I have a friend my age and she's having some trouble."

"Really? What's her problem?"

"She's tired a lot with the grandchildren and all. She can't get fired up."

"How ironic. My college roommate had the same problem until recently. You won't believe it. She got some of that Vagamax at the drugstore. One pill and it's prom night on Blueberry Hill."

"I'll tell my friend about it. What did you say the name is again?"

"It's Vagamax. Your little friend—I mean your friend—is gonna love it."

Women don't see anything funny about getting older, but men relish teasing their friends. I pester Jack about his expanding silhouette as I did when we attended a gathering of forty-year graduates of the University of Tennessee. The group hosted a picnic for about thirty old folks at a campground near Gatlinburg in the Great Smokey Mountains National Park.

We caught up with classmates and socialized until lunchtime. Everyone got a plate. Lines formed on both sides of the table. I noticed one of my colleagues was following Jack through the lunch line on the opposite side of the table. I suggested in a voice loud enough for Jack to hear that the guy might have a better selection if he were in front rather than behind the big fellow.

Jack asserted there was no problem. "After all, I eat like a bird."

"Yeah," I said. "Like one of those prehistoric birds with a forty foot wing span. I believe it was called a pterodactyl. It looked like a giant winged lizard and could carry off a cow."

Jack pretended to be upset by my teasing. "When I say I eat like a bird, I'm talking about a parakeet or maybe a crow." He reminded me that we had traveled to Gatlinburg in his car, and I might need to arrange other transportation back to Knoxville.

I tried to make amends. "Jack, I've always said you have the body of a sixteen-year-old."

"I know what you're going to say—a sixteen-year-old mule."

CARLOS AND RED

"Red is not much of a man, but he's a good friend. Too bad he's so ugly."

"Watch your mouth, Carlos. You're my best pal. But it ain't nothing I'm proud of."

Banter went on all day between two young house painters as they put a fresh coat of white paint on my rambling old house in Ludowici. Red was six-foot-six and weighed no more than 180 pounds. A mop of red hair capped his small head. His thin chin sprouted patchy red whiskers. He looked like a pimento impaled on a toothpick.

Carlos was about a foot shorter, dark and handsome. I enjoyed listening to them, and they loved having an audience.

"Red's not pretty, but I'll say this for him—he's not intelligent either."

"Carlos, let me hear you spell 'intelligent.'"

"Give me a Spanish word, and I'll spell the hell out of it. But you don't know any Spanish words. And not more than a few English words."

I wanted to learn more about these two likeable guys. "Red, how long have you fellows known each other?"

"About seven years, ever since we was in high school."

"Yeah, Red crammed four years of education into five years." Carlos put his brush down and lit a short cigar. "Red and I used to double date. Can you believe a real, live girl ever went out with Red?"

"Hey, I had a girlfriend. She was crazy about me."

"She was crazy all right. I'm not saying Red's girlfriend was a dog, but they had papers on her. When we were driving somewhere, she would hang her head out the window. She would howl at the moon. And you *did not* want to take that girl for a walk."

The conversation halted while I choked with laughter.

"Red, do you remember the time when the four of us were down at Hanes Park and a quail jumped up and flew off? That girlfriend of yours stood on point for two minutes."

"Yeah, but at least I taught her to sit up, roll over and fetch.

135

Tony R. Lindsay

That's more than you ever did with that dizzy skirt you called a girlfriend. Poor girl. I always said she wasn't as smart as she looked. The sad part is she didn't look smart."

"Take it easy, Red. You're talking about my wife."

"You mean ex-wife. It was me she wanted all along, but she had to settle for a short guy. Tell me the truth, Carlos. I bet that when you was in bed with her, she would moan, 'Oh, oh, oh, Red, darling.'"

"Yeah, it happened a couple of times." Carlos was ready to launch another attack. "I remember the night Red took Vickie Ogledorf to our high school prom. Man, even Red couldn't mess up that date. If a guy couldn't score with Vickie, he couldn't score with a whore."

"Not that it's any of your damn business, but me and Vickie got along like cups of a bra. I'd take her to the prom again anytime, but she's married, has twin boys and lives in a big house over in Atlanta."

Carlos and Red were painting window frames. Red complained that Carlos did not know how to properly paint double windows. According to Red, the outside window should be lowered about half way before painting, then raised and the inside window painted.

"You don't know a damn thing 'bout nothing, Carlos. My brother learned me how to paint windows when you was kickin' the slats outta your cradle."

"Well, he *learned* you wrong."

The guys did a nice job on my house. They were finishing up when Red said, "It's a shame that I have to work with a stumpy dude who don't know much about nothing."

"What about me? I have to work with a beanpole without a brain. I get tired of matching wits with an unarmed man."

"What are you saying, Carlos? Are you saying I ain't smart?"

136

OL' DAVE

I snatched up the phone. "Hello."

A middle-aged male voice droned in the world's folksiest drawl. "Is that you, Dan Milino?"

"Yes, who's calling?"

"Dan, this is ol' Dave!"

I was certain this person knew me. We must have been close friends at one time, but I couldn't place the voice. "Dave, please excuse me, but you have me at a disadvantage."

"Hey, that's okay. This is Dave from down at Fit Rite Win-ders and Doors. How y'all doin' tonight?"

I did my best to match his accent.

"Dave, baby, hope y'all boys doin' aw right down at the ol' win-der company?"

"Hey, doin' good. Say, Dan, I hear you's the homeowner out there on Walkertown Road."

"That's right. What's your last name, Dave?"

"Uh, it's Montague."

"What? Are you Purvis Montague's boy? Did your daddy walk with a limp and teach Sunday school at Mount Harmony?"

"Naw, that's somebody else."

"Did you marry that Pittsnogle girl from down around Meager City?"

"Naw, naw. It weren't me."

"That's too bad, Dave. She was good-looking and a real deep breather. You know what I mean?"

"Yeah, I know zackly what ya mean."

"I knew it, Dave. You *did* marry that Pittsnogle girl."

"Naw, naw. Hell naw. I'm just saying I think I know what ya mean 'bout the deep breathin' part. Say, Dan, can we ferget about her fer a minute?"

"I wanted to marry her myself, Davey. But her daddy said I wasn't good enough. You know how that is, don't you?"

"Yeah, sure. Now, about them win-ders."

"What windows?"

"Huh, the damn win-ders in your damn house. Them's the win-ders I'm talkin' 'bout. Sorry. I shouldn't cuss. The boss wouldn't like it. Let me start over."

"Go right ahead. Give me your best shot."

"First of all, you done said you's the homeowner?"

"That's right, Dave, but you got me off the subject before we could talk about the windows."

He covered the phone. After a moment, he was back on the line.

"Say, Dan, about them win-ders. I got a special deal cause we've been workin' out there on Warrentown Road this week."

"It's Walkertown, Davey."

"Yeah, right, that's what I mean. Anyway, we've got a crew out there on your street, and I can give you a real special deal."

"Hey, Davey, you don't mind if I talk with my mouth full, do you? I'm sitting here eating my dinner."

"Naw, naw, it ain't no kind of problem."

"That's good because my wife fixed roast turkey with carrots and peas."

He covered the mouthpiece again. Then, he was back, his voice higher than before.

"First of all, you's the damn homeowner, right?"

"Right."

"And my friggin' name is Dave. You got that?"

"Got it."

"Now then. We got a crew out there on Walkingbird Rd."

"Where?"

"Wherever in hell you sumbitches live. We got a bunch of bastards on your goddamn street. We can come over and give you a fucking estimation."

"Sure, Davey, that would be great. I look forward to meeting you. We can talk about that good-looking, deep-breathing Pittsnogle girl."

"You stupid sumbitch! I ain't givin' you no damn estimation 'bout no damn win-ders or nothing else. And I ain't talking to you about no damn Pitts-slobber girl."

"Pardon me, Dave. It's Pittsnogle."

"I don't care if it's Pitts-shit! I don't care if she looks like a thousand-dollar whore and breathes like a forty-mile fox."

Dave launched into a blistering tirade. According to Davey, I'm descended from a long line of unchaste women.

"I ain't talkin' to y'all about no damn win-ders. Fuck the win-ders. And you can take that stinking turkey, and them carrots, and them slimy peas…."

"Good bye, Davey."

Buzzzzzz.

WONDERING

George told me that he was glad everyone did not have his taste in women. "Otherwise, everyone would want my Mary Jo."

I said nothing, but if everyone had my opinion, *no one* would want Mary Jo.

What kind of trouble would we get into if people could read our minds? Let's say you're chatting away at a dinner party and secretly thinking the hostess has a nice butt. Or, you ask politely for a dinner roll while formulating a plan for relieving the distress in your lower abdomen. Thank goodness no one knows our private thoughts.

***

Did you ever wonder where thoughts originate? What keeps them coming?

At this point, you may be speculating about where my thoughts come from. But let's examine *your* mind. What are you thinking about now, this instant, other than what you are reading? I'll wait while you think about it.

La-deda-de-da-da-da.

La-deda-de-da-da-da.

Okay. You don't have to tell me, but I bet your thoughts are a bit jumbled.

What will you be mulling over two minutes from now? You have no idea, right? That's what I mean. Unless Providence calls you to another life in the next 120 seconds, you will be contemplating something. But we're not in control of our own ruminations. Amazing, isn't it? Anyway, it's just a thought, something to wonder about.

***

If you are an adult, and especially if you are a man, chances are you will think about sex at some point in the next two minutes. After all, sex has universal appeal. Not everyone is interested in baseball, camping, cooking, yellow finches, or blue-tick hounds, but most everyone is interested in sex. A single aspect of life intrigues all of us. You may be thinking that some people have more interest in carnal matters than most folks.

Touché!

Tony R. Lindsay

But we're all interested in sex to some degree, in one way or another, every one of us.

***

I've wondered a lot about atoms. How do such tiny particles know what they are supposed to do and with whom they should associate? Is this is a manifestation of God? Could be, but maybe not.

***

Did you ever wonder how many marvelous people inhabit the world? In our lifetime we will become acquainted with little more than one-billionth of the world's population. Here are three examples of dear people I have read about. They will live and die, and we will never meet them:

A squat, little woman with a unique sense of humor lives in Nepal. If someone falls off a horse, even if they are slightly injured, she laughs until she can hardly stand. She mimics with great exaggeration the rider's ungraceful tumble to the ground. When she laughs, her eyes squint to the point she probably can't see a thing. But we will never have the joy of meeting her. We will not learn about the troubles she has seen or the source of her incredible zest for life.

Ninety-one year old Elmer Redding lives at the Elkmont Assisted Living Center in Indiana. He talks about his son as if the young man were coming for a visit any day. Elmer's son, an Eagle Scout and brilliant engineer, died fifty years ago.

Then there is Brother Mayfield. He is a good man, a preacher, and a closet agnostic.

Life is funny, but it's not easy. And not every story has a happy ending. I wonder what my readers will say about me when I am gone.

Also from Indigo Sea Press:

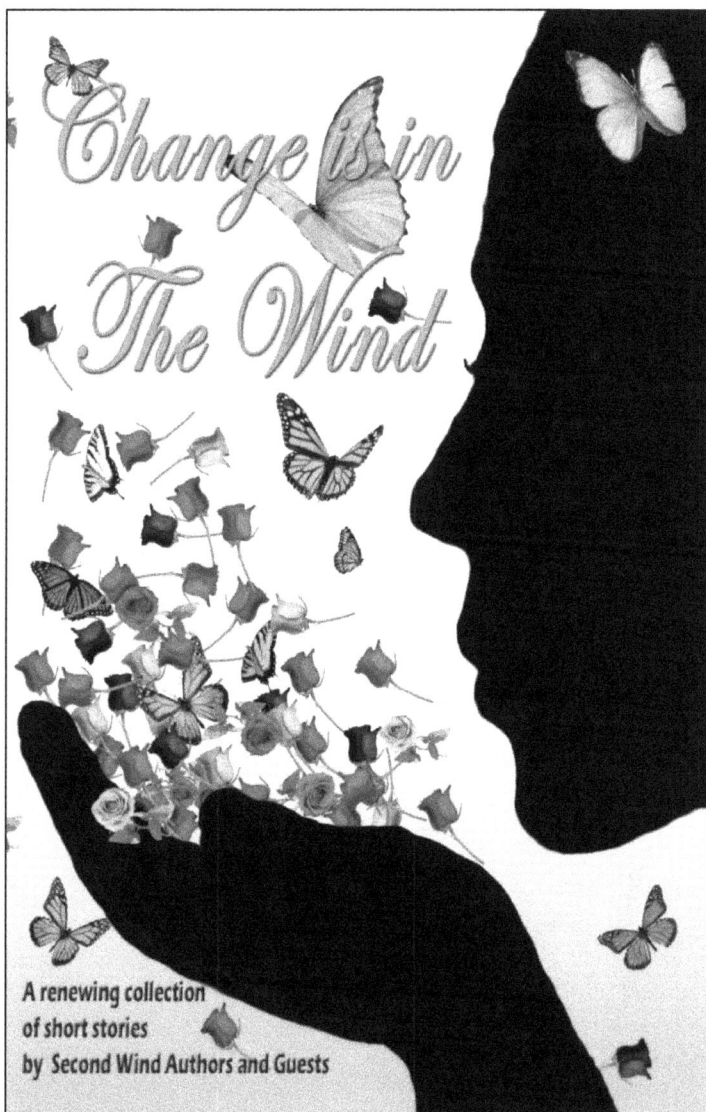

Change In The Wind is a fresh, challenging collection of seventeen short stories by as many authors, all dealing with the theme of change and renewal. Virtually every major theme in modern literature, including romance, mystery, crime, science fiction, religion and even nature find their way into these marvelous, eclectic stories.

The assignment was simple: submit a short story dealing with change. The results were astonishing, engaging, and incredibly varied. The stories compiled in this volume range from taut action drama, to stealthy intrigue, to enthralling spirituality, to tangled relationships, to timeless love renewed—or lost, to angelic second chances. No two of the tales are remotely similar, and yet they are linked in remarkable ways. Each story is tied all the others in the anthology with two exquisite threads. The first constant theme is redemption; in each case there is a transformation, often painful, that brings new beginnings, new possibilities and revitalized life. The second theme is love—timeless and true—expressed in a multitude of ways, but unfailing in bringing hope and newness. *Change in the Wind* is an extraordinary collection of marvelous stories from gifted, eclectic writers who draw us into their worlds and leave us wanting more.